In Their Own Words:

The Abernathy
(Eason, Rivers, and Tarpley)
Slaves of Giles County, Tennessee

Kimberly A. Chase

ANCE**STOR**YBOOK Publishing
Fort Washington

© 2004 Kimberly A. Chase

Publisher's Cataloging-in-Publication

Chase, Kimberly A.
    In their own words: the Abernathy (Eason, Rivers, and Tarpley) slaves of Giles County, Tennessee / Kimberly A. Chase. - 1st ed.
        112 p. cm.
    Includes bibliographical references and index.
    LCCN 2004098628
    ISBN 978-0-9772822-8-9 (pbk. : alk. paper).
    ISBN 978-0-9772822-9-6 (ebook pdf)

    1. African Americans—Tennessee—Giles County—Biography. 2. African Americans—Tennessee—Giles County—History. 3. Giles County (Tenn.)—Biography. 4. Giles County (Tenn.)—Genealogy. 5. Giles County (Tenn.)—History. 6. Slaves—United States—Biography. 7. Slavery—United States—Personal Narratives. 8. United States Colored Troops. 9. United States Army—African American troops—History—19th century. 10. African American soldiers—History—19th century. 11. United States—History—Civil War, 1861-1865—Participation, African American. I.Title

Cover Photo courtesy of the Civil War Photograph Collection, Prints & Photographs Division, Library of Congress, LC-DIG-cwpb-01468

Cover Design by Kimberly A. Chase

Printed in the United States of America

Typeset in Palatino Linotype

First published 2014 by ANCESTORYBOOK Publishing

Individual ebooks may be purchased directly from the publisher's website ANCESTORYBOOK.com . Ebooks and paperbacks may be purchased in quantity by contacting the publisher at sales@ancestorybook.com .

Preface

Through draft or enlistment, an estimated 178,000 African-American men served the Union during the Civil War. Millions descend from these brave souls, yet millions of us are unaware of our familial connection to them due to a lack of oral histories.

In my case for example, my great-grandmother never mentioned that her father and five of her uncles were soldiers in the Union Army. Therefore my grandmother and mother could never share our family's role in America's history with me. Odds are that this same situation has occurred time and time again in the African-American community.

For nearly 10 years, much of my spare time was spent at the National Archives and the Library of Congress researching the genealogy of my family. In January 2004, I was awakened in the wee hours of the morning by a voice delivering my purpose. It was time to dream bigger. It was time to give the forgotten their voice.

I felt compelled to write *In Their Own Words: The Abernathy (Eason, Rivers, and Tarpley) Slaves...* after I found a number of U.S. Colored Troops veterans who were former slaves of the extended Abernathy family in Giles County, Tennessee. It is an account of their lives as slaves in the decades just prior to the Civil War and of their military experiences once they were thrust into a conflict that forever altered their lives.

These men, bonded by circumstance and sometimes blood, were the first to capture my attention through the depositions of their regiment mates, their owners, their families, and of themselves. Because some former slaves and owners bear the same or similar names, the names of all black persons have been bolded for distinction in the text.

With great respect for the struggles they endured, the sacrifices they made, and their contributions to the cause of our freedom, the stories of the Abernathy slaves shall be the first of what could be several "group biographies" published. My hope is that black genealogists who have hit the pre-1870/slavery brick wall will herein find a familiar ancestor and further their research.

My ultimate goal is to glean all genealogically relevant information from the pension files of all veterans of the U.S. Colored Troops and make it readily accessible via database and print format. Alone, this project may take decades. More rapid progress could be made with proper funding, logistical support, and the assistance of equally enthusiastic genealogists.

Enjoy and happy hunting,
Kimberly A. Chase

Contents

I

A Brief History of Giles County,
the Abernathys, and Their Holdings

Before broaching the lives of the Abernathy, Eason, Rivers, and Tarpley slaves, the family who held them in bondage and the evolution of the community in which they were held should be addressed. The core group of Abernathy families in Giles County, Tennessee actually originated in Brunswick County, Virginia where William Abernathy (the son of Charles and Alice) married his wife Elizabeth Clayton. From 1769 to 1790, 9 children were born to the marriage: Clayton Abernathy, Alice Abernathy-Williams, William Abernathy Jr., Jesse Abernathy, Catherine Abernathy-Tarpley, Mrs. Susanna Abernathy, John Abernathy, Elizabeth Abernathy-Drake, and Charles Clayton Abernathy (*see Appendix B*).

For his non-military contributions to the American Revolution, William Abernathy Sr. reportedly received a land grant of 640 acres in Davidson County, Tennessee. In 1808, after one of his sons did some preliminary investigation of that parcel, the Abernathy clan, with the exception of William Jr.'s family, relocated to that parcel at White's Creek near Nashville. A few years later, all but his daughter Elizabeth Abernathy-Drake would settle in newly founded and densely wooded Giles County, Tennessee as planters of corn.[i]

Also kin to the Brunswick County group was Squire Thomas Edward Abernathy, originally of Mecklenburg County, Virginia, who was one of the largest holders of slaves in Giles County, Tennessee. Andrew Jackson Abernathy (born circa 1835) stated, "I remember to have heard my father say that he had never met one of the name whom he could not trace back to this old Virginia source" of two Scottish immigrant brothers.[ii] If this is true, then his father C.C. Abernathy must have included Squire Thomas E. Abernathy. He could not have lived in the closely-knit community and not have known him.

Named in honor of Virginia Governor William Giles, Giles County, Tennessee, also known as "the gateway to Alabama" was formed November 14, 1809 from Native American lands and parts of Maury County, Tennessee. Pulaski, the county seat, was laid off at its midpoint along Richland Creek. Aspen Hill, Bradshaw, Buford Station, Bunker Hill (on Indian Creek), Campbellsville (on Big Creek), Elk Ridge Church, Elkton (on Elk River), old Lynnville (on Lynn Creek), Moriah Church (on Weakley's Creek), and Mount Pisgah were other early communities in Giles County.[iii] The Abernathys mentioned above and their descendants were spread throughout the county, with the greatest concentration in the Pulaski area.

The use of a slave labor force became necessary to their way of life. Although no individual Abernathy held a great number of slaves early on, the family's collective estate of real property and slaves continually grew. In

8

1820, the Federal Census of Giles County, Tennessee reveals 137 slaves owned by the family.

Alan Abernathy (7)

Buckner Abernathy (12)

Burwell Abernathy (14)

Elisha Abernathy (2)

Elizabeth Abernathy (5)

James Abernathy (6)

John Abernathy (7)

John Abernathy (2)

Joseph Abernathy (8)

Sterling Abernathy (3)

Thomas E. Abernathy (10)

William A. Abernathy (7)

Rebecca Harwell (8)

Jason Hopkins (4)

James Paine (28)

William Baker Pepper (2)

Alexander Tarpley (11)

John Williams (1)

49.8% of these slaves were children under the age of 14.

The 1836 Giles County Tax List recorded the following:

Allen Abernathy – 175 acres.

Buck Abernathy – 90 acres, 4 slaves.

Buckner Abernathy – 98 acres, 2 slaves.

Burwell Abernathy (son of Jesse) – 300 acres, 10 slaves.

Charles Clayton Abernathy – 408 acres, 5 slaves.

Colson Abernathy – 148 acres, 1 slave.

D.H. Abernathy – 338 acres, 9 slaves.

David Abernathy – 1 town lot.

Elbert Abernathy – 113 acres.

Elisha Abernathy – 113 acres, 4 slaves.

Hardaway Abernathy – 130 acres.

James Abernathy – 298 acres, 1 slave.

James Abernathy – 3 town lots, 8 slaves.

Jesse Abernathy – 695 acres, 7 slaves.

John Abernathy – 326 acres, 5 slaves.

John Abernathy, Esq. – 4 slaves.

John R. Abernathy – 557 acres, 3 slaves.

John Y.G. Abernathy – 30 acres.

Liles Abernathy – 12 slaves.

Martha Abernathy – 5 slaves.

Mat Abernathy – 2 town lots.
Milton P. Abernathy – 90 acres.
Richard Abernathy (son of Jesse) – 1 slave.
Robert G. Abernathy (son of Susanna) – 135 acres.
Samuel Abernathy – 160 acres, 3 slaves.
Thomas E. Abernathy – 625 acres, 12 slaves.
Wilkins H. Abernathy – 1 slave.
William D. Abernathy – 332 acres, 9 slaves.
Alfred Eason (future son-in-law of Charles C. Abernathy) – 1 slave.
Absolom Harwell (son-in-law of Alice Williams) – 100 acres, 5 slaves
William Baker Pepper (son-in-law of Alice Williams) – 97 acres, 2 slaves
Martha Rivers (future wife of Thomas E. Abernathy) – 500 acres, 14 slaves.
J.M. Payne (future son-in-law of Charles C. Abernathy) – 1920 ac., 25 slaves
Alexander Tarpley (husband of Caty Abernathy) – 462 acres, 3 slaves.
John Williams (son of Alice Abernathy-Williams) – 160 acres, 6 slaves

for a total of 8,400 acres and 166 slaves.

The 1850 Slave Schedules for Giles County reported that the number of slaves held by the Abernathy clan had increased to 236 while their real property carried an estimated value of $86,975.[iv] [v] In 1860, less than a year before the War of the Rebellion would break out, the Slave Schedules of the Federal Census for Giles County counted 357 blacks in bondage to the Abernathy family while the Federal Census reported land assessments of $153,800 and personal property (including slaves) valued at $161,148.[vi] [vii] Individual holdings are as follows (real estate values are bolded):

Alfred H. Abernathy (Circuit Court clerk) in Pulaski: **$5K**/$6525 (4 slaves)
Benjamin F. Abernathy: **$7500**/$6500 (6 slaves)
Burrell Abernathy: (22 slaves)
Burwell Abernathy (farmer): **$18,000**/$26,200 (16 slaves)
Charles C. Abernathy (overseer): **$0**/$1900 (1 slave)
C.C. Abernathy: (1 slave)

Charles C. Abernathy (physician) in Pulaski: (24 slaves)

Colson Abernathy in Pulaski: (34 slaves)

Daniel Abernathy: (8 slaves)

Elisha Abernathy (farmer): **$1620**/$2768 (3 slaves)

Erasmus G. Abernathy (farmer): **$1700**/$1600 (2 slaves)

Ethelbert Abernathy (farmer): **$1500**/$1085

Hartwell Abernathy (farmer): **$7000**/$3085 (2 slaves)

James E. Abernathy: (19 slaves)

John & Caty Abernathy in Pulaski: **$1500**/$5480 (7 slaves)

John Clayton & Mary Abernathy: **$8000**/12,000 (12 slaves)

Mary B. Abernathy: (20 slaves)

R.B. Abernathy: (5 slaves)

Robert G. Abernathy: **$0**/$1557

Robert P. Abernathy: (1 slave)

Sterling Abernathy (farmer): **$10,050**/$625 (1 slave)

Thomas & Martha Abernathy (farmer) in Elkton: **$44,125**/$63,560 (83 slaves)

Turner Abernathy: **$3750**/$2715 (2 slaves)

William Abernathy: (7 slaves)

William A. Abernathy (farmer): **$6375**/$2385 (2 slaves)

William F. Abernathy (farmer & carpenter): **$5500**/$4200 (4 slaves)

William H. Abernathy: (15 slaves)

William J. Abernathy: (2 slaves)

William T. Abernathy (grocer): **$9000**/$1210 (2 slaves)

William T. Abernathy (farmer): **$8000**/$6600 (5 slaves)

Alfred & Mary Ann Eason (farmer) in Pulaski: **$3480**/$6065 (6 slaves)

Gustavus A. Hopkins: (13 slaves)

Ira Tarpley (farmer): (5 slaves)

John Clayton Tarpley (farmer): (18 slaves)

Paschal Tarpley (farmer): **$9000**/$4920 (5 slaves)

Thomas Tarpley (farmer): **$2700**/$168

II

The Abernathy, Eason, Rivers, and Tarpley Slaves - Relations with Their Owners and Their Lives on the Plantation

The Compiled Military Service Records and veteran pension applications of 57 soldiers of the U.S. Colored Troops who served during the Civil War reveal the names and experiences of 87 of the Abernathy slaves. This number is exclusive of the many wives who lived on neighboring farms and the children born of those unions who were the legal property of their mother's owner.

With the exception of 4 young slaves (three males and one female) being gifted to Abernathy heirs, the depositions inside the pension files allude to no overt acts of cruelty (whippings, etc.) on the part of their owners. **George W. Abernathe** (his chosen spelling after the war) was born circa 1845 a slave of Charles Clayton Abernathy. At about age 6, **George** was separated from his mom **Mary**, his brother **James John "Jack"** (born c. 1835), and his sister **Lizzie** (born c. 1840) when Mr. Abernathy gave him to his daughter Mary Ann Eason of Pulaski. She had married before **George** was born.[viii] **James John "Jack" Abernathy** was nearly a man when he fell to Charles Clayton Abernathy's second son, Col. Alfred Harris Abernathy of Pulaski. He remained with him until he joined the Army.[ix] **Tennessee Abernathy-Scales** (born c. 1835), who was the daughter of **Frank**

Abernathy (born c. 1800), and sister of **Foster** (born c. 1846), **Gilbert** (born c. 1844), and **Giles** (born c. 1843), also fell to Col. Alfred Abernathy.[x]

Esic Abernathy, born circa 1847 as **Esic Talley**, did not fare so well. Andrew Jackson Abernathy, the sixth son of Charles Clayton Abernathy, deposed that **Esic** "first belonged to Mister Guilford Talley in Montgomery County, Tennessee and I married Sarah Talley his daughter."[xi] His wife remembered, "…he was a boy and would catch the horses for me before I married and would ride a mule and wait on me… [his] grandmother was our cook and her name was **Sabrina**."[xii]

Esic continued, "[Talley] gave me to his daughter Sarah when I was a child…My father's name was Cunningham. I do not remember his first name. He belonged to Doctor Cunningham in Montgomery County, TN. I do not recall the doctor's first name. He lived in the country half a day's ride from the Tally place…My mother's name was **Lucy**. She belonged to Guilford Tally and bore the name Tally. She died when I was a baby, so did my father…I had brothers **Solomon Tally** and **Isaac Tally**. They lived in Montgomery County, Tennessee on Tally's place…I had sisters **Lucy Tally** and **Philly Tally**. I don't know what became of them."[xiii] His lack of familial bond carried over into his adult life because he never married, had no children, and moved to Colorado. According to **Esic**, "Right after the war I took the name **Albert Cunningham** and have been known as **Al Cunningham** ever since."[xiv]

Unbeknownst to **Esic/Albert**, his brothers continued on at the farm of Guilford Talley until their enlistment.[xv] **Isaac Talley** (born c. 1846) survived the war, but died of smallpox while visiting **Solomon Talley** (born c. 1838) in Illinois. **Solomon** deposed that **Isaac** "came to see me, and I know he was in uniform. I laughed at him for wearing the uniform and told him it was out of date and he told me that Uncle Sam's clothes were never out of date."[xvi]

Like **Esic (Talley) Abernathy**, **Silot Abernathy** (born c. 1842) was born in Montgomery County. Though he never divulges the name of his master, **Silot** is presumed to be part of a dowry for Emily Talley, the sister of Sarah Talley-Abernathy. Emily became the second wife of Gilbert Taylor Abernathy, the oldest son of Charles C. Abernathy. Gilbert and Emily were the only white Abernathy family in Montgomery County, Tennessee in 1860. **Henry Tally** (born c. 1841) who enlisted at Clarksville, Montgomery County, Tennessee as **Henry Abernathy** was most likely a slave of the Gilbert Taylor Abernathy/Emily Talley household.

On the Charles Clayton Abernathy farm, **Lewis Abernathy** (born circa 1838) worked as a house servant and farm hand.[xvii] According to **Columbus "Lum" Abernathy** (born circa 1822), he knew **Lewis** since birth and had him under his supervision.[xviii]   Though his parents' names are not mentioned, **Lewis** did have a large extended family present.   His uncle was the aforementioned **Frank**.   His cousins were **Tennessee, Foster, Gilbert**, and **Giles**.   **Lewis** and his wife **Gracy** (born 1835 in NC) were married in 1862 by **Samuel Brunson** and had one daughter, **Dora** (born May 1864), before the close of the war.   Also at Charles Clayton Abernathy's were **Jesse Abernathy** (born 1845) and his mother **Lucy**.   His father, **Lewis Brown**, lived on a nearby plantation.   **Columbus's** children, **Jefferson (Brunson) Abernathy** (born circa 1846), **Betty** (born circa 1854), **Malinda** (born circa 1856), **Henry** (born circa 1861), and **General** (born circa 1864), along with their mother **Parthenia Brunson** (born circa 1831) were six of the dozen or so slaves of Abdallah Brunson, a blacksmith and planter in Pulaski.

Recording the births of his slaves was a priority for owner Charles Clayton Abernathy. **James John "Jack" Abernathy** recalled, "When I returned to my former master or owner and he recognizing that I was then a free man and would probably go out in to the world for myself, he gave me as he did others of his former slaves who returned with me to our former home a small bible writing there in the date of my birth copying it from his family bible as it was the custom of a great many of the men who owned but a few slaves to make a record of the births of their slaves in their family bibles and that was the custom of my master."[xix]

Colson Abernathy did not record the births of his slaves, but nearly a half of a century after the close of the Civil War, his grandchild J.L. Cardin remembered a slave that Colson brought from Virginia. "I have known **Reuben Abernathy** (colored) all of my life. I will be 65 years of age in August 1914. **Reuben** is 6 or 7 years older than I am. He belonged to my grandfather Colston Abernathy, but there was no record kept of his age. He was a good plow-hand when he was a very small boy."[xx]

Martin Abernathy was a slave of Colson Abernathy as well. His wife **Silloy** (born circa 1820-1828) was a slave of James M. Bass of Bunker Hill, as were their nine children: **Harriet** (born 11/20/1846), **Mary Frances** (12/18/1847), **Caroline** (born 3/23/1849), **Eliza Jane** (born 7/24/1851), **Sarah** (born 7/25/1854), **Burrell** (born 4/27/1856), **Priestly** (born 2/24/1858), **Walter** (born 12/31/1861), and **Robert** (10/11/1864). **Martin** and **Silloy** were married Christmas Eve 1845 by John Bonner at the residence of Nathan Bass.[xxi]

Reese Abernathy (born circa 1842) was also a slave of Colson Abernathy since early childhood. At his enlistment, **Reese** is described at 5'2" with a copper complexion. In Bunker Hill at a neighboring farm, **Reese** found his future wife **Prudence** (born circa 1841). Also known as **Martha**, she was one of six slaves belonging to widow Martha Osborne. With their owners' permission, **Reese** and **Prudence** were wed in 1859 by William Myers at the Osborne farm. Although she was 18 when she married, **Prudence** had already bore 3 children (**Samuel**, **Rachel**, and **Spencer**) by men whose names were not given. Together **Reese** and **Prudence** had 4 daughters: **Dolly Ann (Osborne) Abernathy-Young** (born 2/2/1860), **Narcissie (Osborne) Abernathy** (born 10/13/1862), **Mary Abernathy** (born 1865), and **Jennie Abernathy**.[xxii]

Doctor "Dock" Abernathy (born circa 1831) was the son of **Edward** and **Phebe** (born circa 1798), and one of only two slaves owned by Turner Abernathy. **"Dock"** became the second husband of **Ann (House) Bass** (born c. 1820) and stepfather to the 3 children she had with **Frank Daniel**: **Mary**, **Constantine**, and **Columbus**. James Bass, the husband of **Ann's** second owner, confirmed, "Her second husband was **Dock Abernathy**, who belonged to Turner Abernathy, a near neighbor of mine. They had no ceremony, not any regular marriage, but they lived together as husband and wife on my place and they were so recognized by me and my wife."[xxiii] Children from that marriage were **Jane Bass** (born 4/1845, died 3/1864), **Isabelle Bass** (born 5/1849, died 1853), **Milton Bass** (born 9/4/1851), and **Delilia Bass** (born 10/10/1847) who married **John Rivers**.

Other Abernathy slaves in Giles County whose individual owners have not been identified include the following (all born in Tennessee unless noted otherwise, birthdates are approximate):

Abraham (1857), son of Major
Abram (1822 in Va)

Albert (1845)
Alfred (1853)

18

Anderson #1 (1844)
Anderson #2 (1853)
Andrew (1861)
Ann (1860), daughter of Francis #1
Angie (1840 in Va)
Argen (1805 in Va)
Austin (1807 in N.C.)
Benjamin Wiley (1845)
Branch (1857), son of Argen
Buckner (1849), son of Major
Caroline (1840), daughter of Julie
Champ (1825 in Va)
Charles (1800 in N.C.)
Daniel (1842)
Danthula (1859), daughter of Angie
David #1 (1840)
David #2 (1858)
Davy (1825 in Ga)
Dick #1 (1840)
Dick #2 (1855)
Easter (1848), daughter of Major
Edy (1801 in Va), wife of Stephen
Eli (1840 in Ga)
Fountain (?), son of Mary #4
Francis #1 (1843), dau. of Austin
Francis #2 (1845)
Frank #1 (1837)
Frank #2 (1844)
Frank #3 (1853), son of Major
Franklin (1800), husband of Mary #1
Frederick (1817)
George #1 (1820 in Va)
George #2 (1850)
George #3 (1863), son of Francis #2
George #4 (1864), son of Major
Grannison (1846), son of James #1
Harriet (1818), wife of Wash
Harrison #1 (1844)
Harrison #2 (1845 in Va)
Harrison #3 (1848 in Va)

Hartwell (1815 in Va)
Henry #1 (1807)
Henry #2 (1834)
Henry #3 (1846)
Henry #4 (1857), son of Caroline
Henry #5 (1857), son of Molsey
Isabelle (1858), sister of Nelson
Isham (1854)
Jack (1815)
James #1 (1809)
James #2 (1819), son of Lucy #1
James #3 (1825)
James #4 (1840)
James #5 (1849)
Jeff (1862), son of Major
John #1 (1845), son of Mary #3
John #2 (1853), son of Thom
John H. (1842)
Joseph (1837)
Julie (1800 in Va)
Kissy (1800 in Va), wife of Wm #1
Lethia (1851), daughter of Mary #5
Lethy (1825)
Lillie (1862), daughter of Sarah
Lou Ann (1853)
Lucy #1 (1788 Va)
Lucy #2 (1853 in Va), dau. of Argen
Luis (1830)
Mahala (1819 in Md)
Major (1818)
Mary #1 (1800), wife of Franklin
Mary #2 (1814)
Mary #3 (1821), m. of John & Susan
Mary #4 (1824)
Mary #5 (1825)
May #1 (1853)
May #2 (1855)
Mildred (1854)
Milly (1820)
Molsey (1818 in N.C.)

Monroe (1842)
Moses (1813 in Va)
Nelson (1851), brother of Susan #1
Peter (1830)
Polly (1858), daughter of Major
Reuben B. (1848)
Rhoda (1852), daughter of Mary #5
Richard (?)
Robert (1844)
Rubin (1822 in Va)
Ruff (1845)
Sam (1844 in Va), son of Argen
Sarah #1 (1838)
Sarah #2 (1864)
Sherrell (1846 in Va)

Sophia (1858), daughter of Molsey
Squire (1851)
Stephen (1800 in Va)
Susan #1 (1848), sister of Isabelle
Susan #2 (1851)
Sylvester (1844)
Thom (1825), father of John #2
Thomas #1 (1827)
Thomas #2 (1830)
Tony #1 (1820)
Tony #2 (1851 in Va), son of Argen
Wash (1813), husband of Harriet
William #1 (1800 in Va)
William #2 (1832)
William Sylvester (?)

Few of the Tarpley slaves are known by name: **Austin** (born c. 1837), **David** (born c. 1840), **Henry** (born c. 1830), **Henry** (born c. 1841-1845), **Melissa** (born c. 1838), **Monroe** (born c. 1846), and **Wesley** (born c. 1833). **Henry Tarpley's** master was Tom Ira Tarpley. Though technically still a slave, **Henry Tarpley** married **Agnes Lock** on 3/14/1865 while still on active duty in the Army.

The owners of brothers **Austin** and **Wesley Tarpley** has been identified as Clayton Tarpley. In his pension file, **Austin Tarpley** stated that his father was **Frank Abernathy**.[xxiv] An older woman named **Mary** (born c. 1820) living with him in 1870 is presumed to be his mother.[xxv] **Monroe Tarpley's** mother was **Harriet Foster**.

Elder **James Brunson** wed **Melissa Tarpley** and **Frederick Abernathy** (born c. 1817) on December 11,

1854. They had only one child which died the same day it was born in September 1855. Both **Austin** and **Wesley Tarpley** married slaves from the adjoining Buchanan plantation at Weakley's Creek. Mrs. Sarah Buchanan, **Jane Lucinda Buchanan's** mistress, deposed, "**Wesley** and **Jane** were married by ceremony, according to the slave custom, at my house, but I do not recollect who said the ceremony."[xxvi]   On November 17, 1855, **Anderson Buchanan**, **Jane's** uncle, officiated the wedding. The children born to them were **Mary Elizabeth Buchanan** (born 1857) and **Jessie Idella Buchanan** (born 1860). **Austin Tarpley's** first wife was **Mary Buchanan**. Their son **William Tarpley** was born circa 1868.

In 1838, Thomas E. Abernathy married Martha Paine-Rivers, the widow of William Rivers, and from that day on until the war, he was the largest holder of slaves in the family. According to James Rivers, Martha's son from her first marriage, the Rivers slaves "became the property of my stepfather Thomas Abernathy and by that means they took the name of Abernathy instead of Rivers."[xxvii]

Henry Abernathy (born c. 1797), a Rivers-Abernathy slave, spoke highly of his owner, "Tom Abernathy was a good master to all slaves, giving [me] $5 to $10 at a time."[xxviii]   **Gordon Abernathy** (born c. 1839) was a stepson of **Henry Abernathy**. He was gifted to Burrell Abernathy by his father Thomas. **Gordon** maintained affable relationships with his current and former owners

21

as he was given permission and "visited his mother on Tom Abernathy's place nearly every Sunday."[xxix]

Great leeway was given to **Henry Abernathy**. His first wife was **Mason**, and their children were **Rebecca**, **Nancy**, **Fayette**, **Robert**, **Mira**, and **Ned** (born c. 1846). **Mason** also had 4 children prior to marriage: **Tom**, **Louisa**, **Jennie**, and **Sophia**. His second wife **Margaret** brought her 2 sons, **Gordon** and **Tyler** (born c. 1841) to the marriage. All benefited from **Henry Abernathy's** role as a favorite. He was put in charge of the field hands after his right shoulder and leg were injured "by a young horse dragging him about the yard."[xxx] **Sarah Abernathy** was often sent by their master to rub his side with "some instrument."[xxxi]

Wesley Rivers (born c. 1842) remembered, "After **Henry** got hurt, he was made a sort of boss by Master Tom, [he] had to wake up the hands [and] look after the hands in the field. He was always bossing the other slaves and worked the same as the rest, but after he got hurt he did not have to plow or do any kind of hard work."[xxxii]

His injury did not hinder his sideline enterprises. **Sarah** reminisced, "**Henry** always had a nice watermelon patch, would sell a good many and generally worked them on Saturday afternoons" and that she had "seen him drive his children out of it fearing they would wither the vines. There were a good many sugar trees on

Master Abernathy's place. [He] always made sugar and syrup for the master and for himself, [but he'd] have to make his share at night. All of **Henry's** children would help him at it."[xxxiii] He even enlisted his stepson **Gordon** to help him sell sugar and watermelons.[xxxiv] "When **Ned** got old enough to work he was employed about Master Tom's house, carrying water, chopping wood, and other chores. He also worked in the fields for 3 or 4 years before he went in the army," **Henry** deposed.[xxxv]

Also at the plantation of Squire Tom Abernathy was **Robert Abernathy** (born circa 1819). He married **Amanda Goods** on December 16, 1844 at her owner Esquire Goods' place. **Amanda** eventually became the slave of Dr. Charles N. Ordway, a planter in Elkton. **Robert's** children **James Ordway** (born 9/16/1842), **Martha Mitchell** (born 10/1848), **Ann Abernathy** (5/17/1852), **Maria Sloss** (born 3/12/1854), and **Watkins Abernathy** (born 2/11/1856) also belonged to Dr. Ordway. **James** however was permitted to work alongside his father. In his 1890 deposition, **James** stated, "My father was a blacksmith by trade and I was his striker at the time."[xxxvi]

Alfred Rivers (born 1825) and his wife **Nancy** came under the ownership of James W. Rivers at the beginning of the war. They were originally slaves of Bill Huey of Columbia, Maury County, Tennessee and then went through a series of owners, Mr. Dobbins and William Rivers of Mississippi. To avoid Federal troops that were removing slaves from plantations, William Rivers sold or sent many of his across the Tennessee River to James W. Rivers in Giles County.[xxxvii] Other slaves of James W. Rivers include **John Rivers** (born c. 1840), **Burrell Rivers** (born circa 1823) who married his wife **Maria Brown** (born circa 1832) at the Rivers plantation in Giles County on December 2, 1849, and their children **Frankie** (born 11/3/1853) and **Nelson** (born 12/26/1858).[xxxviii]

Born in Giles County, **Henry Rivers** (born circa 1829) and his wife **Isabella Flournoy** (born circa 1845, died 6/4/1899) were married in 1862 by **George Powell** in Mississippi before being sent across the Tennessee River once again with their baby boy **Henry**.[xxxix] His mother **Charlotte Rivers** (born c. 1800 in VA) and his sister **Francis Rivers** (born c. 1840 in TN) resided with him in 1870.[xl]

Isabella's mother **Jane Rivers** (born circa 1817) also went through a series of owners. The first, Dr. Kemp of Virginia, came to Elkton, Tennessee. His daughter Martha Flournoy of Pulaski was next. The third set of owners were Julia (Flournoy) and William Rivers. **Jane Rivers** trekked across the Tennessee River twice with her other children **Washington Rivers** (born c. 1841), **Julia**, **Martha** (born 1/1849), **David Rivers** (born 3/1850), **John H. Rivers** (born 5/1851), and **Laura Rivers Powell**. All children except **Laura** were fathered by **John (Mayo) Flournoy**, who died in 1853. [xli]

Other River slaves included:

Adaline (1857), dau. of Cinda
Alfred (1840), brother of Nancy
Alonzo (1840), son of Braxton
Braxton (1813), hus. of Lucinda
Cinda (1830), mother of Elizabeth
David (1830), husband of Fannie
Eliza (1851), daughter of Braxton
Elizabeth (1854), dau. of Cinda
Fannie (1830), wife of David
Francis (1851), dau. of Harrison
Harrison (1837)

Isaac (1844), son of Braxton
Jack (1835), father of Martin
James (1840)
Lea (1845), daughter of Braxton
Louisa (1854), daughter of Nancy
Lucinda (1820), wife of Braxton
Martin (1861), son of Jack
Nancy (1832), sister of Alfred
Sackey (1850), son of Braxton
Silas (1838), son of Braxton
William (1814)

By 1840, the second daughter of Charles Clayton Abernathy, Mary Ann, had married Alfred Eason of Pulaski. In turn, Eason's holdings expanded from 0 acres and 1 slave in 1836 to $2,000 in real estate and 7 slaves in 1850.[xlii] Long time Pulaski resident **Ralph Holt** deposed, "I remember a white man named Alfred Eason who lived about 5 miles from Pulaski and who owned some colored folks. One of the colored men was **George Washington Eason** [who] served in my company."[xliii]

Of those 7 slaves, six have been identified: **George Washington Eason** (born circa 1830), **Mary (Abernathy) Eason** (born circa 1823), and her children **Frank Eason** (born circa 1840), **Harry "Henry" Eason** (born circa 1843), **Peter Eason** (born circa 1846), **George W. Eason**, and an infant girl (born circa 1850). **George W. Abernathe** (born circa 1845) deposed that he did not go to the Easons until age 6. Maria Abernathy-Payne, older sister of Mary Ann

25

Abernathy-Eason, first owned **George Washington Eason**. **Edmond Killion** deposed, "I knew his parents. His father was **Frank Abernathy**, he belonged to a different white man."[xliv] His mother's first or last name was **Washington**.[xlv]

Joe Long has been mentioned as **Mary (Abernathy) Eason's** husband.[xlvi] Of **Mary's** sons, only **Frank Eason** and **George W. Eason** could have been fathered by **Joe Long**. In Civil War veteran pension claims filed on behalf of **Mary's** sons, the father of **Frank Eason** is not identified. **Balam McNairy**, who died in 1865, was identified as **Peter Eason's** dad.[xlvii] **Harry "Henry" Eason** was fathered by Alfred Eason, the husband of his mother's owner.[xlviii]

Patience (Freeman-Tarpley)-Eason-Meredith (born circa 1844) said of her husband, **Harry** was almost white, a very light mulatto…he was the son of his master and was given a great deal of liberty."[xlix] The lack of restrictions placed upon **Harry Eason**, especially regarding his frequent visits to **Patience**, was obvious to all who knew him. "I don't remember that he ever asked permission to come and see her. I had no objections to his coming for he was a good darky and always behaved himself…**Patience Meredith** was formerly a slave in my family. I raised her from [the] time she was four years old…," recalled Mary N. Tarpley.[l] **Patience** was born on the Elkton farm of Reuben Freeman and became the slave

26

of his daughter. **Patience** stated, "I was a house girl and was carding and spinning [thread]."[li]

"I first met the soldier **Henry Eason** about 3 years before his enlistment and that was about 3 miles from Pulaski, Tennessee on the farm of Mr. & Mrs. William and Mary Tarpley…I was duly married to him by a slave marriage without the usual formal ceremony but by and with the knowledge and consent of both of our owners to the same and by our mutual and constant cohabitation thereafter 'til his enlistment," **Patience** recalled.[lii]   She also stated, "My mistress said she had only one objection and that she was afraid my children would be white."[liii]

Luke Freeman, another slave of Mary N. Freeman-Tarpley, confirmed the relationship, "I know that they certainly slept together. He would usually come on Saturday nights and Sundays and sometimes Wednesday nights and at other times."[liv] **Mary Scales-Eason-Kimbro** (born circa 1835) corroborated **Patience's** allegations of marriage, "She and I married brothers.   She married **Henry Eason** and I **Frank Eason**."[lv] At the William Scales farm on December 5, 1857, **Sam Brunson** wed **Mary** to **Frank Eason**. Their daughter, **Harriet (Scales) Eason** was born in March 1864.

Oddly enough, Susannah Connell, the daughter of Mary Ann Abernathy and Alfred Eason and the slightly younger half-sister of **Harry "Henry" Eason**, was candid in her recollections, "**Harry Eason** and [**Patience**] were

27

not married, but they were recognized as lovers and we all thought they would marry. We used to tease them... He went to see her regularly, usually whenever he wanted to."[lvi]

On the other hand, relations between Mary Ann Abernathy-Eason and her slave **Mary (Abernathy) Eason** were strained to the point that the former had no choice but to sell the latter. Once again, **Patience** shed light on the situation, "I knew **Harry Eason's** mother, **Mary Eason**, when I was a girl. She was sold away to a man named Bonner in Goadville. She never came back to this country after she went away."[lvii] The time period of the sale of **Mary (Abernathy) Eason** to Mr. Bonner can be narrowed by the 1860 Federal Census Slave Schedule where an adult female slave is no longer present with the Eason family where she had been reported in 1850 and 1840.[lviii]

While the instances of mixed race/ethnicity persons was as common as slavery in the southern plantation culture, **Harry "Henry" Eason** seems to be the only slave owned by the extended Abernathy family who was outed as a child of his master. However, because of the number of mulatto slaves owned by the family, it is possible that some were fathered by their masters or other male visitors to those farms.

The 1860 Slave Schedules of Giles County, Tennessee reported the following:

Slave owner	#Slaves/Mulattoes	Age/Sex of Mulattoes
Alfred H. Abernathy	4 Slaves/1 Mulatto	(12) Female
Burrell Abernathy	22 Slaves/13 Mul.	(70)F, (45)M, (35)F, (24)M, (17) F, (14)M, (12)F, (10)F, (8)F, (6)F, (4)M, (2)M, (1 m)M.
Burwell Abernathy	16 Slaves/3 Mulatto	(26)M, (11)M, (7)F.
Ch. C. Abernathy	24 Slaves/5 Mulatto	(68)F, (55)M, (36)F, (16)F,(8)F.
Colston Abernathy	34 Slaves/5 Mulatto	(17)F, (13)F,(12)M, (9)M,(7)M.
James E. Abernathy	19 Slaves/1 Mulatto	(18)F.
John G. Abernathy	5 Slaves/1 Mulatto	(11)M.
Mary B. Abernathy	20 Slaves/9 Mulatto	(45)F, (35)F, (20)F, (15)F, (13)M, (4)F, (2)M,(2)F,(2 m)M.
Robert P. Abernathy	1 Slave/1 Mulatto	(17)F.
Thom. E. Abernathy	83 Slaves/8 Mulatto	(35)F, (22)F, (18)F, (14)F, (13)M, (12)M, (10)F, (5)F.
Turner Abernathy	2 Slaves/1 Mulatto	(61)F.
W.L. Abernathy	5 Slaves/1 Mulatto	(5)F.
W.T. Abernathy	2 Slaves/1 Mulatto	(50)F.
Alfred Eason	6 Slaves/1 Mulatto	(15) M.
James W. Rivers	38 Slaves/1 Mulatto	(14)F.
John C. Tarpley	18 Slaves/1 Mulatto	(25)M.
Nancy E. Tarpley	4 Slaves/2 Mulatto	(10)M, (7)M.

Fifty-five mulattoes were recorded as slaves of the extended Abernathy family in 1860. The standard by which the term "mulatto" was applied in the 1860 Slave Schedules for Giles County, Tennessee is puzzling. Slaves such as **Esic (Talley) Abernathy**, whose medical examination required for his veteran's pension described him as having a "dark yellow" complexion, failed to be recorded as mulatto when the slaves of Sarah Talley and Andrew J. Abernathy were reported.[lix] Neither **Henry Rivers** nor **John Rivers**, both veterans with yellow complexions, were accurately described in the 1860 Census. It is as if only the slaves with the fairest of complexions were to be reported as mulattoes.

III

A Call to Arms – Organizing the Regiments

"Liberty won by white men would lack half its lustre. Who would be free themselves must strike the blow. Better even to die free than to live as slaves. This is the sentiment of every brave colored man among us."
-Frederick Douglass

The idea of war over the issue of states' rights germinated in Southern minds nearly two decades before a shot had been fired. A call to action, secession from the Union, was brought before the Southern constituency. On February 9, 1861 Tennessee initially rejected the referendum, but President Abraham Lincoln's call for troops and the firing upon Fort Sumter were the catalysts causing the state's secession on June 8, 1861.

Prior to this, the Emancipation Proclamation had declared free all slaves residing in states of rebellion. Tennessee had not seceded from the Union, neither had parts of Virginia nor southern Louisiana; therefore those slaves remained in bondage. They were forced to bide their time until Federal troops fanned across the South and made their way to their doorsteps.

When President Lincoln issued the executive order allowing the draft and voluntary enlistment of Negroes into the Union military forces, tens of thousands would answer the call. Confederates conceived of punishments for black soldiers and their commanding white officers if captured.

From August 1863 through mid-February 1864, the following black regiments were organized in Tennessee:

- 12th United States Colored Infantry *(originally known as the 3rd Tennessee Volunteers [African Descent], a.k.a. the 1st United States Infantry[Colored])* at Elk River Bridge and Nashville

- 13th United States Colored Infantry *(originally known as the 2nd United States Infantry Regiment [Colored])* at Elk River Bridge and Nashville

- 14th United States Colored Infantry at Gallatin

- 16th United States Colored Infantry at Clarksville and Nashville

- 110th United States Colored Infantry *(originally known as the 2nd Alabama Colored Infantry)* at Richland Station, Butler's Ford, and Pulaski

- 111th United States Colored Infantry *(originally known as the 3rd Alabama Colored Infantry)* at Pulaski and Richland Station

The enrollment for confirmed/presumed Abernathy, Eason, Rivers, and Tarpley slaves was as follows:

12th USCI (comp.)

Esic Abernathy (C)
Gilbert Abernathy (C)
Jesse Abernathy (C)
John H. Abernathy (E)
George W. Eason (C)

13th USCI (comp.)

Anderson Abernathy(F)
George Abernathy (D)
(James) Monroe " (D)

14th USCI (comp.)

Henry Abernathy (B)
James John "   (H)

16th USCI (comp.)

Frank Abernathy (D)
Henry Abernathy (D)
Silot Abernathy (F)

??? USCI

Amos Abernathy

110th USCI (co.)

Albert Abernathy (F)
Ben Wiley " (D)
Daniel Abernathy (B)
Doctor Abernathy (F)
Fountain Abernathy (?)
George W. (Green) " (K)
Grant Abernathy (D)
Harrison Abernathy (E)
Jeff (Brunson) " (F)
John Randall " *(D)
Martin Abernathy (F)
Monroe Abernathy (F)
Ned Abernathy (K)
Thomas Abernathy (F)
Tyler Abernathy (F)
William (Reese) " (F)
William Sylvester " (I)
Henry Rivers (B)
Wash Rivers (B)
Wesley Rivers (K)
Austin Tarpley (G)
Moses Tarpley (G)
Wesley Tarpley (G)

111th USCI (co.)

Foster Abernathy (G)
Frank Abernathy (B)
Frank Abernathy (C)
Fred Abernathy (G)
Giles Abernathy (I)
Henry Abernathy (G)
Lewis Abernathy (G)
Manuel Abernathy (G)
Reuben Abernathy (G)
Richard Abernathy (G)
Robert Abernathy (A)
Tony Abernathy (G)
Frank Eason (G)
Henry Eason (E & G)
Peter Eason (G)
Alfred Rivers (D)
Burrell Rivers (D)
Harrison Rivers (D)
John Rivers (D)
Robert Rivers (D)
David Tarpley (G)
Henry Tarpley (G)
Monroe Tarpley (A)

In July of 1863, Union forces swept through Giles County farms and according to **Esic**, "Grant's army came and got all able-bodied Negroes, myself among them. I was willing to go…**Amos Abernathy** went from our place. So did **Jeff Abernathy**. **Amos** died after the war."[lx]   Although he was a slave of the Brunsons, **Jefferson (Brunson) Abernathy** seems to have spent considerable time at the plantation of his father's owner's daughter.

No pension application of any kind was filed on behalf of **Amos Abernathy**; therefore the particulars of his family and servitude are unknown. **Amos** did not serve under the surname of Abernathy. The name he enlisted under is unknown. Had it not been for the deposition of **Esic**, **Amos's** existence and connection to the Abernathy family would have remained unknown. However there was an unapproved widow's pension claim filed by **Bettie Adams** of Tennessee on behalf of soldier **Amos/Abe Adams** who reportedly served in both the 12th and the 110th U.S. Colored Infantries.

Esic's mistress Sarah Talley Abernathy remembered, "He and a boy **Lewis** each took a mule and left our place in Giles County, Tennessee in wheat threshing time… They took up in camps with the Federal soldiers, [and] were corralled. I never heard if he joined the army."[lxi] **Esic** enrolled immediately on August 1, 1863, but despite leaving the farm at the same time, **Jefferson** would not join until December 9, while **Lewis** waited until January 20, 1864.

Also in Pulaski, Federal troops drafted slaves from the farm of Mary Ann Abernathy and Alfred Eason. **Harry "Henry" Eason's** widow **Patience (Freeman-Tarpley) Eason-Meredith** stated, "He was taken from the field of his master Alfred Eason by the soldiers, but I cannot tell you what year it was…he was working in a piece a 'new ground', at work plowing. It was about the time the Union men first came into this country."[lxii]

Down in Elkton, slaves of Thomas E. Abernathy also left with Federal soldiers. **James Oddway**, the son of **Robert Abernathy**, recalled, "My father and I enlisted together the same day at Richland, Giles County, Tennessee in Company A, 111th U.S. Col'd. Troops...and served as regular soldiers in our company."[lxiii] "For the examination we had to strip stark naked," claimed **Reuben Abernathy**, a Virginia-born slave of Colson Abernathy.[lxiv] **James J. Abernathy** echoed a similar experience, "When I enlisted I was carefully examined, being stripped and sounded. This was at Gallatin, Tenn. There were others examined at the same time."[lxv]

After their organization, men from the 12th U.S.C. Infantry remained at Elk River Bridge as guards while they drilled and were instructed. With forethought, the white commanding officers of some black regiments saw the importance of not just military training, but of education as well. "Our first colonel was Sullivan whose wife was a schoolteacher and taught the men in the army ...We were not cavalry, but mounted as scouts," deposed **Esic Abernathy** (Co. C, 12th USCI).[lxvi] **George Washington Eason** (Co. C, 12th USCI) recalled, "We were at Elk River about a year when we left and went to Nashville, TN from there to NWRR near Sulphur Springs [and] worked the road."[lxvii]

On November 3, 1863, the 12th U.S.C. Infantry reported for duty in Nashville at the Nashville & Northwestern Railroad (N&NWRR). It was ordered extended from Nashville to Johnsonville, so that supplies could be shipped upriver to Johnsonville and then taken by rail to Nashville. Two hundred men of the 12th USCI worked on this project through its completion in May 1864, while the remaining soldiers engaged in guard duty along the railway.

The 13th U.S.C. Infantry also supplied 50 men as construction workers for the N&NWRR and afterwards was assigned to guard a portion of it. The 14th U.S.C. Infantry went to Chattanooga in February 1864 to work on fortifications. In mid-March, Colonel Thomas J. Morgan took the 14th USCI on a recruiting expedition. He was ordered not to impress more Negroes into service, but to take along any whom freely wished to join. Many slaves returned with his forces to Chattanooga. The 14th USCI was later detailed to garrison duty and wagon train protection between Chattanooga, Tennessee and Dalton, Georgia.[lxviii] After its organization, the 16th U.S.C. Infantry was also sent to Chattanooga for fortifications work.

After all were mustered into active duty, the 110th & 111th U.S.C. Infantries followed similar paths, garrison duty at Pulaski followed by guard duty along the N&NWRR in northern Alabama. **James Oddway** (Co. A, 111th USCI) explained, "From Richland our company and some 5 other companies of our regiment were sent to Sulfur Trestle R.R. Bridge, Limestone County, Alabama."[lxix] Once there, his father **Robert Abernathy** (Co. A, 111th USCI) worked as a blacksmith, wagoner, and teamster.[lxx]

Sulphur Branch Trestle Fort was a small installation near Sulphur Branch Creek in Elkmont, Alabama. For communications and the transportation of their troops, functioning railways held great importance to the Union army. The fort at Sulphur Branch was constructed by the Union to defend the area's trestle bridge for the Nashville and Decatur Railroad. The garrison inside the fort consisted of both black and white soldiers. 111th USCI member **Jonas Mark** said, "The Co. remained 2 or 3 months and then, during the summer of 1864, we went to Athens, Alabama."[lxxi]

The fort at Athens, Alabama was desegregated as well. The 3rd Tennessee Cavalry and the 18th Michigan Infantry were two of the white Union regiments camped there. **Lewis Abernathy** (Co. G, 111th USCI) recalled, "My Co. was detailed to garrison Athens, AL. There were there also 5 companies of the 110th Regiment. We remained at that place until sometime in September 1864."[lxxii]

IV

Daily Military Life - Reminders of Home, Non-Combat Injuries/Fatalities, and the Beginning of an Epidemic

The daily routine of a soldier is never easy with a constant reminder of all comforts and liberties denied. A hot meal, a cool drink, and a straw mattress bed inside a scarcely appointed slave cabin are imaginably more preferably than sleeping upon the hard and dewy ground after consuming army-issued hardtack.

Initially colored soldiers received $7 per month wages, nearly half of what white privates were being paid. In protest some would tear up their pay stubs, but it was not a dissention to be taken lightly. Now wage earners, these former slaves had families looking to them for financial support, especially if they were to vacate the plantation. By June 20, 1864, a retroactive pay increase equaling $16 per month for privates, black or white, took effect. $576 after a 3-year tour of duty was still a tidy sum for a colored soldier, but with furloughs few and far between, homesickness was a contagion for which temporary "desertions" were a drastic cure. Visitors and messages from home provided the mental sustenance to go on just a little while longer.

Thomas Watkins recalled meeting the mother of Private **Monroe Tarpley** (Co. A, 111th USCI), "…She came to see him and stayed with him, he acknowledging and introducing her as his mother. She remained with him as long as they remained in camp, but was not allowed to go with the regiment when it moved."[lxxiii]

Soldier **Frank Reed** remembered, "While the company was camped near Pulaski, a woman named **Martha** came there to see **Reese** and she claimed him as her husband and he as his wife."[lxxiv] Private **Reese Abernathy** (Co. F, 110th USCI) enlisted under the alias of **William Reese**. The wife **"Martha"** was actually **Prudence Osborne-Abernathy**. **Martha** was probably her Christian name.

Brothers **Frank** and **Harry "Henry" Eason**, both of Co. G, 111th USCI, received visits from their wives. **Frank's** widow **Mary Scales-Eason-Kimbro** recalled, "When they encamped here at Pulaski, **Patience** and I both came up here and she stayed up here with him, and I stayed with my husband."[lxxv]

Henry Abernathy also paid the 110th U.S.C.I. a visit at "…Athens, Alabama to see his son **Ned** [and] took him some milk and cornbread and pies."[lxxvi] **Ned** sent his father a few dollars by way of Sergeant **Wesley Rivers** (Co. K, 110th USCI) who returned home to the Rivers plantation after deserting the army.[lxxvii] **Neil Brown** and **Smith Reynolds**, both of Giles County, swore in their deposition that **Ned** "…did in part support **Henry Abernathy** from the spring of 1863 up to his enlistment in the army [and] that [**Ned**] always considered it his duty to aid and assist him to as great an extent as lay in his power."[lxxviii]

At Sulphur Branch Trestle Fort, a mysterious shooting death happened on March 12, 1864. Private **Peter Eason** (Co. G, 111th USCI) was assigned to picket duty the night before. **Tony Abernathy** and **Lewis Walker** (both of Co. G, 111[th] USCI), both deposed, "We know that he went on post at 9 o'clock and the following morning at 7am whilst on post was killed. We never heard that it was accidentally, he was shot ____ ____, the regiment believed that he was killed by a bushw[h]acker. We further testify that we saw his dead body brought in when the Company carried him in the morning and laid before the Captain's door."[lxxix] For over 9 years, members of the 111[th] U.S. Colored Infantry believed this falsehood. The truth could have hurt the camaraderie of the soldiers and cast a suspicious eye on the actually shooter. A letter to the Adjutant General's office stated without further explanation that **Peter Eason** was "accidentally shot by private **Fount Jones** of Co. G, 3rd Alabama Infantry A[frican]. D[escent]."[lxxx]

In April of 1864, Private **George W. Abernathe** and the remainder of Company D of the 13th USCI had come off guard duty at the Northwestern Railroad and returned to Camp Thomas when a most unlikely occurrence took place. According to **George**, "[While] cleaning up our guns in camp, one [soldier] of the company was on the inside of the log tent or cabin, and was punching his gun against the wall trying to get his

41

ramrod out." **George** further explained that "he was on [the] outside of the cabin when [a] log fell down from the top on his head, and knocked him down and [he] was taken into the tent or cabin in an unconscious condition…".[lxxxi] His comrade **Benjamin Jordan** recalled "him unconscious for the time, for 3 or 4 hours. He was not sent to the hospital but cared for in camp."[lxxxii]

Corporal **Henry Gray** remembered, "It was the discipline of our company during the service in the late war to require the soldier to go and answer to his name at 'Roll Call' each time, even though the soldier was sick, confined to quarters, and unable to attend at 'Roll Call'. He was necessarily forced to be present and answer to his name, although he was not required to do soldier duty, if excused by the surgeon of company or regiment."[lxxxiii] Captain William Duncan added, "…it was nothing unusual in the Co. and Reg. named for a man to be sick and ailing and yet answer his name at Roll Call and be current on the roll as present for duty. The discipline in the Regiment and Co. was very severe and if a man could crawl, he had to get out. This is why so many of the enlisted men have such poor Hospital records."[lxxxiv]

Private **Austin Tarpley** (Co. G, 110th USCI) also had a freak accident. He recalled, "Our Company was on a march toward Atlanta, Georgia during the summer of 1864. In passing through a swamp, it became necessary to build a corduroy road for the wagons to pass over said swamp. I was carrying a piece of timber and as I stooped over to place said timber, one of my comrades who was carrying another piece of timber threw the same upon my arm and broke one bone of it."[lxxxv] During a similar march from Chattanooga, Tennessee to Rome, Georgia, Private **Daniel Abernathy** of Company B was reported deserted on October 6, 1864.[lxxxvi]

Illness is synonymous with war, and the War Between the States was no exception. From the regimental hospitals and prisons, to the contraband camps and depleted plantations, diseases such as measles, smallpox, cholera, and dysentery spread like wildfire and claimed thousands of lives. The first Abernathy casualty was Private **Anderson Abernathy**, a soldier in Co. F, 13th USCI. He was just 19 years old when he enlisted on September 28, 1863 and died less than 2 months later on November 14, 1863 as he hemorrhaged from his bowels. It was not stated what illness or injury caused his death.[lxxxvii] No pension claims were filed on his behalf.

Private **Grannison Abernathy** enlisted as **Grant Abernathy** in Co. D of the 110th U.S. Colored Infantry on December 8, 1863 in Pulaski. One month and 8 days later, he died of pneumonia at the Pulaski Government Hospital without a chance to see the world outside of Pulaski. **James Abernathy** (born 1809) filed a dependent father's claim in 1868, but it was rejected, probably because **Grannison** had not served able-bodied for the minimum of 90 days.[lxxxviii]

In late January 1864, Musician **Jefferson (Brunson) Abernathy** (Co. F, 110th USCI) seemed to have been the first black Abernathy soldier with measles, but from whom he contracted it is unknown. **Jefferson** stated, "I was first in [the] hospital with measles soon after enlistment at Athens, Alabama. Before I was fully able for duty I was taken with smallpox and sent to [the] hospital again. This was during the first winter of my enlistment."[lxxxix] Private **Reuben Abernathy** (Co. G, 111th USCI) also contracted smallpox after suffering from measles.

The first measles death was that of Private **Foster Abernathy** (born c. 1846) of Company G, 111th U.S.C. Infantry on April 11, 1865 at Sulphur Branch Trestle in Alabama.[xc] Private **Reese Abernathy** alias **William Reese** (Co. F, 110th USCI) was the second to succumb to the disease, dying May 10, 1864 in Athens.[xci] **Baylor Watson**, a company mate of **Reese** who also witnessed his nuptials, remembered that he "saw him when he was taken to the hospital. [I] saw the measles when it broke out on him and the Doctor of the Regiment said it was the measles he had and he died while in the Hospital."[xcii] The measles epidemic was on its way to becoming full blown, but one soldier was responsible for bringing it back to the plantation.

Private **Lewis Abernathy** (Co. G, 111th USCI) spoke of his being homesick, unaware at the time that he was infected, "I was doing duty, but [I] was puny and I asked Capt. Daniel [McTaggart] to let me go home for awhile, but he refused. I wanted to come home and see my wife and so I left anyway. I was gone about 2 months."[xciii] The Company Muster Roll for May/June 1864 marked **Lewis** as "deserted".[xciv]

Tennessee Abernathy-Scales's memory of the situation was, "I understood from neighborhood talk, that he was very sick with the measles, and that if it had not been for his wife and mother he would have died. He was out of his head, and did not know anybody. It was also said that he went back to his company before he got entirely well. I understood that some of his company came after some other soldiers who had come home, and that they took **Lewis** along. I saw him only once and that was the day the soldiers took him off. I did not speak with him, he passed close by me, he looked very sick and was nothing but skin and bones."[xcv] **Tennessee's** husband **Merritt Scales** deposed, "The measles spread on the Abernathy place among the blacks and whites and Mr. Abernathy and his wife took them, and 3 of the colored people died after [**Lewis**] got there on the Abernathy place: **Archy**, **Fountain**, and **Roeny**."[xcvi]

Lewis confirmed his arrest, "I was picked up at home by some scouting parties and turned over to my company at Athens, AL. I was not tried for desertion. I returned about July 1864.[xcvii] The July/August 1864 Company Muster Roll stated the following about **Lewis**: "recovered from desertion July 22nd, in confinement and charges preferred."[xcviii] A court-martial was pending.

During General William Sherman's march to the sea, Private **Washington Rivers** (Co. B, 110th USCI) was admitted to the hospital in Rome, Georgia where he died July 1, 1864 of brain fever.

Private **Doctor "Dock" Abernathy** (Co. F, 110th USCI) took sick with an undisclosed illness in April 1864 and died September 1, 1864 at the Pulaski Gov't. Hospital. [xcix]

The deposition of **Willis Malone**, a private in Company D of the 111th U.S. Colored Infantry, revealed that Private **George W. Abernathy** alias **George W. Green** also contracted the measles in September 1864 at Athens, Alabama.[c]

There may have been 2 or 3 different men with the name **Fountain Abernathy**, each with different dates and places of death. In 1899, a **Mary Mitchell** (born circa 1824) applied for a dependent mother's pension for her son **Fountain Abernathy**. He was reportedly a member of the 110th U.S. Colored Infantry who died December 7, 1864 in Pulaski of fever and dysentery. At the date **Mary Mitchell** pinpointed as her son's death, a great portion of the 110th and 111th were in Mobile, Alabama. There is also the **Fountain** who died of measles on the Abernathy farm. If **Fountain Abernathy** performed any duty for the military, it was under an alias. Considering his unusual name, he could have been the Private **Fount Jones** who accidentally shot Private **Peter Eason**. The mystery shall remain one because **Fount Jones's** original military records were lost. The meager information in his file revealed his enlistment at Pulaski and his death at Gainesville, Mississippi on October 15, 1864.[ci] No pension claims were filed on his behalf.

For the 12th and 13th U.S. Colored Infantries, casualties of enlisted men due to disease were 242 and 265 respectively. However, illness was just the beginning for these soldiers. With death and disease surrounding them, the 12th, 13th, 14th, 16th, 110th, and 111th U.S. Colored Infantries were about to come face to face with the true nature of war.

V

The Wages of War - Clashes with the Rebels, Battles Scars, and Prisoners of War

"When General Thomas rode over the battlefield and saw the bodies of colored men side by side with the foremost, on the very works of the enemy, he turned to his staff, saying 'Gentlemen, the question is settled. Negroes will fight.'"

-Thomas J. Morgan, Colonel of the 14th USC Infantry

War, often a necessary evil to evoke real change, can be a cruelty that knows no bounds. In an era when some Confederates loss their riches, their land, and their way of life, human decency was gone. The 110th and the 111th U.S. Colored Infantries to which most of the former Abernathy, Eason, Rivers, and Tarpley slaves belonged were especially hit hard.

Not a battle had been fought. Not a shot had been fired. Nine months had passed since the first wave of Abernathy slaves had enlisted in the Union Army. Their first skirmish would come on May 13, 1864 in Pulaski, Tennessee where the 111th USCI tended to garrison duty. The 110th USCI saw its first fight in Dallas, Georgia on May 31, 1864. As part of the Atlanta Campaign, the Battle of Dallas (also known as New Hope Church or Pumpkinville Creek) took place from May 26 to June 1. Fighting ensued after Lt. General William J. Hardee's troops searched the Union's defensive line for weaknesses. The Rebels were repelled with 3,000 casualties versus the 2,400 lost by the Union.

On August 14, 1864, the 14th USCI and other regiments marched from Chattanooga, Tennessee to the Dalton, Georgia blockhouse which they found under attack by Confederate Major General Joseph Wheeler's Cavalry. Wheeler had raided northern Georgia to destroy railroad tracks and supplies. In the late afternoon of August 14, he demanded the surrender of the garrison at Dalton. Col. Bernard Laibolt, commander of the garrison, refused. Fighting ensued and the Union troops retreated to the outskirts of town where they held out at hillside fortifications. Heavy combat continued throughout the night and Wheeler's Cavalry withdrew on August 15 after the 14th U.S.C. Infantry participated in the charge to drive the rebels out. Casualties for the Battle of Dalton, Georgia were 1 killed and 2 wounded. Thomas J. Morgan, Colonel of the 14th USCI reported, "The conduct of the entire regiment was good. It was its first encounter, and it evinced soldierly qualities; the men were brave, and the officers cool."

On September 14, 1864, the 16th U.S. Colored Infantry was ordered to destroy all ferryboats while patrolling the Tennessee River, return to Chattanooga, and keep Wheeler's Cavalry from crossing it. The 16th USCI saw no action until September 26, 1864 when for 3 days it was involved in multiple skirmishes with General Forrest's troops in Pulaski after the Confederates destroyed portions of the railroad along the way.

The forces of Confederate General Nathan Bedford Forrest were in Athens, Alabama on September 24. Though the Union fort atop Coleman Hill was heavily armed and populated, General Forrest wanted control of it before Union reinforcements could arrive. After making their presence known with a barrage of gunfire, General Forrest convinced the fort commander, Colonel William Campbell, to meet outside with him at the Rebel camp. Sergeant **Wesley Rivers** (Co. K, 110th USCI) remembered, "I received wounds in my left leg and right shoulder, from a piece of shell while in action in the Battle of Athens, Alabama about September 1864."[cii]

Though the Confederate regiment was significantly smaller than the Union garrison inside the fort, Forrest and his men pulled the biggest ruse over on Campbell. A well-choreographed tour of the camp, a game of "smoke and mirrors" with soldiers and cannons, and a boastful declaration on the futility of a battle was all the persuasion Col. Campbell needed to return to the post, lower the flag, and surrender the fort without an additional shot being fired. Knowing Col. Campbell would keep a running tally of the enemy troops surrounding the fort, Forrest's men had repositioned themselves elsewhere to be counted again and again.

One major, 2 captains, and 5 lieutenants of the 3rd Tennessee Cavalry who were also taken prisoner at the fort signed a statement of protest against the unjustified surrender. With at least a week's worth of ample provisions (water, food, and ammunition) on hand, the surrender was unnecessary. Estimates of more than 1,400 Union soldiers were taken prisoner on that day in Athens. Former Abernathy, Eason, Rivers, and Tarpley slaves who were captured that day in Athens, Alabama included:

Albert Abernathy (F, 110)	Tony Abernathy (G, 111)
Frederick Abernathy (G, 111)	Tyler Abernathy (A, 110)
George W. (Green) " (K, 110)	Frank Eason (G, 111)
Henry Abernathy (G, 111)	Harry Eason (E & G, 111)
Jeff (Brunson) Abernathy (F, 110)	Burrell Rivers (D, 111)
Lewis Abernathy (C, 111)	Harrison Rivers (D, 111)
Monroe Abernathy (F, 110)	John Rivers (D, 111)
Ned Abernathy (K, 110)	Wesley Rivers (K, 110)
Richard Abernathy (G, 111)	David Tarpley (G, 111)
Thomas Abernathy (F, 110)	Henry Tarpley (G, 111)

The capture of the fort at Athens, Alabama could be viewed as fortuitous for **Lewis Abernathy** (Co. G, 111th USCI) because the Company Muster Roll of September/October 1864 stated he was "captured at Athens, Alabama September 24, 1864 while in confinement awaiting sentence of court-martial for desertion."[ciii] His original sentence may remain a mystery, but sometimes executions were an extreme punishment for desertion.

Alongside Private **Lewis Abernathy** in the Athens Fort guardhouse was Private **Alfred Rivers** (Co. D, 111th USCI) who according to the Company Muster Roll was "in confinement awaiting trial for desertion" in

July/August 1864, but his "whereabouts [were] unknown since September 24, 1864." **Alfred** either escaped from prison or evaded capture by the Confederates all together, as he was reported back to duty March 4, 1865.[civ]

Pushing northward, General Forrest's troops opened fire on the Sulphur Branch Trestle Fort in the early morning hours of Saturday, September 25, 1864. The fort commander Colonel Lathrop and many others were killed. **Henry Tarpley** (Co. G, 111th USCI) deposed, "My first colonel, Colonel Lathrop was killed in the latter part of September 1864 at Sulphur Trestle, Alabama. He was killed on Sunday. I with nearly the entire regiment was captured the day before our colonel was killed by General Forrest."[cv] Caught off guard, the remaining Federal soldiers surrendered. The fort and trestle bridge were torched. Several hundred soldiers were taken prisoner including companies of the 110th and 111th USC Infantries. Abernathy and Tarpley slaves captured at Sulphur Branch Trestle Fort included:

Frank Abernathy (B, 111th USCI)   Reuben Abernathy (G, 111th USCI)
Frank Abernathy (C, 111th USCI)   Robert Abernathy (A, 111th USCI)
Giles Abernathy (I, 111th USCI)   Monroe Tarpley (A, 111th USCI)

As promised by the Confederacy, black soldiers taken as prisoners of war were forced into manual labor while their white officers were shipped to Castle Morgan, the Confederate military prison in Cahaba, Alabama. Though better treated than the majority of white POWs in the Civil War, hundreds of those sentenced to Castle

Morgan Prison would not survive their boat ride home once paroled. They were victims of the Sultana disaster on April 27, 1865.

James Oddway, who served beside his father **Robert Abernathy** in Company A of the 111th U.S.C. Infantry, recalled, "We were captured on a Sunday morning about 3 o'clock. That same morning all the prisoners were put en route towards Mobile, Alabama under guard of Col. Logwood's _____ Rebel Cavalry. My father and I and **Peyton Black**, the latter of Company C, also prisoners, were taken out from among other prisoners, and my father and **Black** were assigned to the blacksmith shop of Col. Logwood's regiment to shoe the rebel horses and I to wait on Capt. Buchanan, Robert Buchanan I think, of Co. A same regiment and to take care of his horses."[cvi] The Company Muster Roll of the 111th USCI makes the first mention of Robert Abernathy's separation from the rest of the regiment.[cvii]

The 110th and 111th U.S. Colored Infantries and their captors relocated often along the Tennessee River. Private **James Oddway** continued, "While at Florence, AL during the movements of the rebel cavalry my father came to me one morning before daylight, and told me that he and **Peyton Black** had determined to make their escape from the rebels that morning and he wanted me to go with them. I told him that it would be a risky undertaking, that there would be too many soldiers about and that we would be killed if discovered in the attempt to escape. My father told me then that the cavalry was going to cross the river to the South side and he thought it was a good chance, while that was going on to escape. I told him finally that I did not care to risk it, and so he left without me. He also told me that **Peyton Black** was waiting for him a short distance in the woods outside the picket line. When my father left, he went in a northerly direction from our camp and he had scarcely been gone 4 or 5 minutes. I heard 5 or 6 reports of guns in the direction my father had gone, which at once satisfied me that my father had been killed and I remarked to Captain Buchanan…that they had killed my Daddy. He said no, but that they had taken him to Mobile, Alabama, that he had tried to get away, and that he had been caught in the act…I hear[d] nothing about my father nor did I know anything about **Peyton Black** until I met him again at Murfreesboro. I then asked **Black** what had become of my father. He then told me that my Daddy had been killed while he was making his way back to him, after he left me the morning of their escape. He said that he saw the rebels shoot him and, I think that they threw his corpse in the Tennessee River."[cviii]

The 1890 deposition of **Peyton Black** revealed his memory of Private **Robert Abernathy's** last moments alive. "The wagon trains and troops of Forrest's cavalry had been ordered back to Corrinth, Mississippi. That night **Robert** and myself made up our minds to make our escape, if we could, and about 9 or 10 o'clock in the morning we both left camp near Perryville for the purpose of making our escape, but **Bob** did not want to go without his boy, **James**, and he went to see him with a view of getting him to join us. While **Bob** was going toward his son's camp, I was dodging in the woods trying to hide from the rebels who were all around there. I think **Bob** had gone about 200-300 yards from the time we separated, when I heard the reports of 2 guns and somebody cry out 'Oh!' and from that I presumed, **Bob** had been shot. The shots were fired in the direction **Bob** had gone. I never saw him again."[cix]

Months after the Regiment's release from Rebel prison, the September/October 1865 Company Muster Roll branded him a deserter because he "never rejoined his command."[cx] However, with the help of the above depositions, **Robert Abernathy** was vindicated. The following notation was put in his records on October 7, 1890: "It has been determined from the records on file and evidence brought before this department that the charges of absences without leave and desertion against this soldier are erroneous. He is supposed to have died, exact date and cause unknown on or about October 15, 1864, while in the hands of the enemy."[cxi]

Private **Reuben Abernathy** (Co. G, 111th USCI) described an experience that was typical of many colored soldiers who became the Confederate Army's prisoners of war, "We were captured by General Forrest's rebel cavalry in the Fall of 1864...where all the prisoners were put to work on the rebel fortifications and obstructions of the harbor or bay. We were obliged to work. The rebels put us to work, it was no choice. It was compulsion. If any of us had refused to work they would have worn us out with a leather strap or switch…I was unloading large heavy piles from a flat-boat and setting the piles upon end for the steam pile driver to drive down in the bottom of the Bay. The piles were about 3 feet round measure and about 40 ft. long. They were of pine lumber, very heavy and bad to handle on the water."[cxii] His comrade **Lewis Abernathy** swore to **Reuben's** injury, "The labor being very severe precipitated an unusual strain resulting in an umbilical hernia."[cxiii] **Reuben** also revealed the unsanitary conditions inside the prison, "My bladder trouble was caused by drinking muddy water in said prison, which I was compelled to do or else die from thirst."[cxiv]

About his forced return from desertion, **Lewis Abernathy** deposed, "I was out in the guardhouse and was there when captured by Forrest's cavalry. All the colored prisoners of war, myself included, were forced to work on the rebel fortifications. If we had refused, they would have lashed us; They lashed us because they had the power to do so. I received many a lick I did not deserve, when at work. We were confined in a regular prison pen, i.e. in the ___ when the 'nigger-traders' used to put slaves to keep them from running away. We had good houses – brick houses, but little covering for the night and bad food…We were shielded, at night against the rain and bad weather, but in the daytime we had to take it as it came…They had no mercy on a black soldier

...They took our uniform[s] away from us at Athens when we were captured, except our pants."[cxv]

Private **John Rivers** (Co. D, 110th USCI) echoed the inhumane treatment they received, saying he had been "greatly exposed and whipped by Rebels."[cxvi] Sergeant **Henry Tarpley** (Co. G, 111th USCI) recalled, "I suffered an injury of [the] right knee made with a hatchet by one of the enemy while I was a prisoner. He threw the hatchet at me on a boat in Alabama."[cxvii]

Willis Malone deposed on behalf of Private **George W. (Green) Abernathy** (Co. K, 110th USCI), "He was with me, a prisoner at the time. He worked first on the breastworks, then out in the water driving piles and planting torpedoes for the confederates."[cxviii] Musician **Jefferson (Brunson) Abernathy** (Co. F, 110th USCI) stated, "They put us to building breastworks in wet ground and water and I was not used to such rough treatment...While working as a prisoner of war in the confederate breastworks, after being all day in the water, we would come out of the ditches at night and slept in our wet clothes on a mussel shell floor without a shred of covering."[cxix] **Peter Kinder** gave an affidavit as to the illness of **Monroe Abernathy** (Co. F, 110th USCI) stating that he "was a member of [**Monroe's**] regiment and [he] was captured to Mobile, Alabama and [**Monroe**] contracted camp fever...in prison from exposure and bad treatment...the camp fever settled in [his] legs and hips and chest."[cxx]

Inside of Rebel Prisons, deaths from disease, exposure, and mistreatment were common and some slaves of the extended Abernathy family fell victim to the deplorable conditions. Captain Daniel McTaggart (Co. G, 111th USCI) made the following statement about **Frederick Abernathy**, "I certify on my honor that Private **Fred Abernatha**, Co. G, 111th US Colored Infantry, died at Maridian, Mississippi while in prison on the 1st day of March 1865 and that from the best of my knowledge and belief his death was caused by inhumane treatment received from the enemy."[cxxi] **Frederick Abernathy** was 47 years old when he enlisted, much older than most soldiers.

Thomas Butler and **Tyler Abernathy**, both of Co. F, 110th USCI, swore, "We were personally present at the death and inhumation of…**Martin Abernathy** who… died of general debility combined with a severe cough, properly speaking 'pulmonary consumption' which he contracted whilst a Prisoner of War at Mobile, Ala."[cxxii] A former slave of Colson Abernathy, **Martin Abernathy** died leaving his wife **Silloy Bass** with 9 children.

Other victims of "exposure" and "cruel treatment from the enemy" in the Mobile, Alabama Confederate Prison included:

Burrell Rivers (Co. D, 111th USCI), age 41, died 12/15/1864 of pneumonia

Harry "Henry" Eason (Co. E & G, 111th USCI), age 21, died 12/25/1864

Richard Abernathy (Co. G, 111th USCI), age unknown, died 2/12/1865

Frank Eason (Co. G, 111th USCI), age 25, died 4/5/1865

With all odds against them, some black prisoners of war did manage to escape. **Wesley Rivers** (Co. K, 110th USCI) stated that he "was a prisoner about 3 hours when he escaped, came to Pulaski, reported to General Dodge, was assigned to duty at Pulaski, and rejoined [his] regiment after the Hood raid at Kingston Springs, TN. The company to which [he] and **Ned Abernathy** belonged had not returned from prison. [He] never saw **Ned** after he was taken prisoner."[cxxiii]

Although taken prisoner at Athens, **David Tarpley** (Co. G, 111th USCI) seemed to have escaped and rejoined his command, because in January 1865 he was assigned to temporary duty with Companies H and K of his regiment.[cxxiv] The same can be said of **Monroe Tarpley** (Co. A&C, 111th USCI), who from February to May 1865 was member of a detachment arresting deserters in Pulaski.[cxxv]

Slaves such as **Robert Abernathy** (not of Co. A, 111th USCI) did not have the opportunity to enlist in the Union Army because they were obliged to serve their masters away at war. **Robert Abernathy**, brother of **Thomas Abernathy** (Co. F, 110th USCI), deposed, "I was in the Confederate Army with my master. I saw my brother when he was a POW at Mobile, Alabama."[cxxvi] Their master was Squire Tom Abernathy.

In the listing for Tennessee Colored Pension Applications for the Confederate States of America was one **Ruff Abernathy** who was born in Giles County,

Tennessee. He claimed service with the 3rd Tennessee Infantry and his claim was approved for payment. His pension file is held in Tennessee, therefore the true identity, family, and possible owner are a mystery to the author. If **Ruff Abernathy** remained in Giles County after the Civil War, he may be the **Rufus Abernathy** (born c. 1845) in the 1870 Federal Census.

On October 27, 1864, the 14th USCI came under attack in Decatur, Alabama while it was en route to Nashville, Tennessee to relieve Col. Charles C. Doolittle's forces and fight General John Bell Hood's Army. **Payne Harris** of the 14th USCI deposed, "It was just a while before the Hood fight at Nashville and while we were going on to that fight."[cxxvii] As part of the Franklin-Nashville Campaign, the siege of Decatur lasted from October 27 to 30, 1864. Hood's Army of Tennessee demonstrated against Decatur and then attempted to cross the Tennessee River. On the 28th, the 14th USCI charged, carrying an enemy battery, spiked its guns, and captured 14 prisoners. With only 5,000 men, the Union Army halted the much larger grouping of Rebels from fording the Tennessee River, resulting in a Union victory. The 14th USC Infantry's casualties in Decatur were: 2 killed, 52 wounded, and 1 missing.

James John "Jack" Abernathy of Company H discussed how he was wounded in the attack, "It was in the fall of '64 that my leg was injured. It was in Decatur, Alabama while engaged fighting Hood [that] a ball from a gun struck me in the left leg just above the ankle. I was then carried to the rear, put in an ambulance, and sent back on the train to the hospital...It was **Wash Carmon** who carried me to the train on the ambulance...I went back into camp but did no active duty for 2 weeks. The bone in my leg was shivered. I walked lame then and ever since."[cxxviii]

"I saw him [the] same day he was shot. He was able to walk around. He was sent from the company to the hospital at Nashville...The shot went through the leg like he had been standing with his side to the direction [from which] the bullet came. The bullet went in on [the] outside of the leg and out on the inside or the opposite, and 3 or 4 inches, above [the] ankle. After he came back to us from [the] hospital, he was as spry as ever except he limped a little on that leg, and at times, especially in rainy weather he complained of it hurting him," **Payne Harris** concluded.[cxxix]

Major General Robert S. Granger praised the 14th USC Infantry reporting, "The action of the colored troops under Col. Morgan was everything that could be expected or desired of soldiers. They were cool, brave, and determined; and under the heaviest fire of the enemy exhibited no signs of confusion."

After the completion of the Johnsonville extension for the N&NWRR, part of the 13th USC Infantry remained at Johnsonville, Tennessee and was attacked by General Nathan Bedford Forrest's forces during the first week in November. Engagement reports show some of the men of the 13th USCI armed with Enfield rifles, were stationed along the riverbanks of the Tennessee as sharpshooters and performed well. During their guard duty along the N&NWRR, the 12th USCI saw action on November 24, 1864 at Buford's Station on Section 37 of the railway. On November 30, the 13th and 16th USC Infantries were ordered to Nashville. Along the way, the 16th USCI was engaged in daily skirmishes and a member of Company B killed a civilian living near Murfreesboro Pike, but no incident report is available.

When the 14th USCI left Chattanooga en route for Nashville, Companies A and D were among those troops riding the troop train on the Nashville & Chattanooga Railroad. Near Mill Creek, the train was fired upon and derailed by one of General Forrest's batteries at Stockade #2. Under fire for many hours, the 14th USCI suffered multiple casualties (2 killed, 5 wounded, 18 missing) and left for Nashville with the fall of darkness.

Following a defeat and tremendous losses in Franklin, Tennessee on November 30, General John Bell Hood was determined to expel General William T. Sherman's army out of Georgia. He led the Army of Tennessee northward to Nashville. By December 1, various segments of Maj. General George H. Thomas's Union Army had already reached Nashville, Tennessee. Unbeknownst to General Hood, an equally determined Thomas had planned for this inevitable battle for 2 weeks with the intention of destroying the Army of Tennessee.

On December 2, Hood and his forces arrived on the outskirts of town, occupied positions on a line of hills parallel to those of the Union, and commenced to erecting fieldworks, while the 12th USCI skirmished near Clarksville, Tennessee. The Union Army would use fortifications already in place since 1862. Due to ice and freezing rain, fighting was delayed. On December 15, 1864, The Battle of Nashville commenced upon a muddied cornfield and lasted two days. The 12th, 13th, 14th, and 16th USC Infantries were present, however the 16th USCI saw no action at the battle because it was assigned to guard a pontoon bridge at Rutherford Creek. Striking the Confederate left and right, all attacks against rebel positions were eventually successful.

Once again, **James J. Abernathy** was injured. He described, "[I] went to Nashville, Tennessee and took part in the battle. I know this was in the fall but can't say in what month. It was in that engagement that a fragment of a shell struck my gun that I was then holding at an aim. It knocked the gun against my left arm and my arm was stiff ever since."[cxxx] **George W. Eason** (Co. C, 12th USCI) received a gunshot wound to the left arm.[cxxxi] The fighting stopped at nightfall, but both Union and Confederate troops worked to construct new fieldworks at Shy's and Overton's Hills.

That morning, the Union's initial attack at Overton's Hill failed. Major Gen. George H. Thomas reported, "Our men moved steadily onward up the hill near the crest, when the reserve of the enemy rose and poured into the assaulting column a most destructive fire causing the men to waver and then fall back, leaving their dead and wounded, black and white indiscriminately mingled – lying amid the abatis."[cxxxii] In the second line of that assault, the 13th USCI pushed forward when the front lines faltered. Some soldiers were able to climb the embankment that protected the Confederates from Union gunfire, but they were forced to retreat.

Monroe Abernathy (alias **James Monroe**) stated "that at Overton Hill about 5 miles south of Nashville, Tennessee about the 16th day of Dec. 1864, while making a charge upon Rebel lines under [the] command of Hood [I] received a bullet wound from a mini musket I think, on the inside of [the] left ankle, said wound cutting some of the _____ and nerves of my foot."[cxxxiii] Captain William Duncan (Co. D, 13th USCI) spoke of **Monroe's** gunshot wound "which disabled him from performing further immediate duty and I ascendingly ordered him back to the Hospital to Nashville, TN for treatment."[cxxxiv]

The 14th USCI did not charge up Overton's Hill, but protected the artillery. The battle report of Colonel Morgan stated, "Lieutenant Col. Corbin, 14th US Colored Troops, does not possess sufficient courage to command brave men. Captain Baker in reality commanded the 14th Regiment on the 15th and 16th, and acquitted himself with good credit."

The assault on Shy's Hill was a success, inspiring other Union Troops to charge Overton's Hill once again, that time with victorious results. Hood's Army of the Tennessee retreated, fleeing through the only escape route left open by General Thomas. The 12th USCI with other Union regiments gave chase and for 10 days pursued the beaten and battered remnants of General Hood's men through Brentwood and Franklin, forcing them to re-cross the Tennessee River into Decatur, Alabama on December 27, 1864. The 12th USCI was the first regiment to cross behind Hood's Confederate army. A sharp engagement there resulted in the loss of 3 officers and 10 men. The 12th USCI returned to Nashville, Tennessee on January 9, 1865. Also on January 9, a detachment of the 110th USCI was in Larkinsville, Alabama, although no explanation for their purpose there can be immediately found.

The Army of Tennessee was disintegrating, with men dying of cold and famine, deserters fleeing in all directions, and over 4,400 casualties and Prisoners of War at the Battle of Nashville. Thoroughly humiliated, General John Bell Hood retreated to Tupelo, Mississippi and resigned his command. During the pursuit of Hood's army, Private **Gilbert Abernathy** (Co. C, 12th USCI) took sick with an undisclosed illness, was sent to Huntsville, Alabama, and died March 14, 1865 in Hospital #16 in Nashville, Tennessee.[cxxxv]

In reference to the casualties of the Battle of Nashville, Corporal **Esic Abernathy** said, "I do not recall the names of any who were killed. There were many. I was in two heavy battles, of which I remember only one

_____ with General Hood at Nashville, TN."[cxxxvi]   In the course of those 2 days of battle, the 12th USCI lost ¼ of their regiment in casualties: 13 killed, 102 wounded, and 6 missing. The 13th USCI suffered a 40% loss of soldiers with 55 killed, 165 wounded, and 9 missing. The 14th USCI casualties were 4 killed, 41 wounded, and 20 missing. The 16th USCI had 1 killed in action and 2 wounded.

Maj. General James B. Steedman, a commander of the Union Army at the Battle of Nashville, reported, "The larger portion of these losses, amounting in the aggregate to fully 25 per cent of the men under my command who were taken into action, it will be observed fell upon the colored troops. The severe loss of this part of my troops was in their brilliant charge on the enemy's works on Overton Hill on Friday afternoon. I was unable to discover that color made any difference in the fighting of my troops. All, white and black, nobly did their duty as soldiers, and evinced cheerfulness and resolution such as I have never seen excelled in any campaign of the war in which I have borne a part."[cxxxvii]

After his injury in the Battle of Nashville, Sergeant **James John "Jack" Abernathy** recalled, "I was then off duty nearly 5 months, was in camp at Chattanooga and did no duty and was not under treatment, simply carried my arm in a sling. The next duty I did was help to dig up dead men at Missionary Ridge and Lookout Valley and burying them in the cemetery. This was about the close of the war in '65. It was while doing this work that

67

I contracted smallpox and was carried to the hospital at the foot of Lookout Mountain. It was a smallpox hospital and every morning they carried out 50 or 60 men that had died from the disease. I don't know anybody that was there. There was only one beside myself from our regiment that ever got out alive that I know of. I cannot recall his name."[cxxxviii]

The war had been raging for 4 years without an immediate end in sight. The Federal Government realized the success of the Union Army following the recruitment of colored men and needed a new influx of soldiers. The March 3, 1865 Joint Resolution of Congress read:

"Resolved by the Senate and House of Representatives of the United States of America in Congress assembled, that, for the purpose of encouraging enlistments and promoting the efficiency of the military and naval forces of the United States, it is hereby enacted that the wife and children, if any he have, of any person that has been, or may be, mustered into the military or naval service of the United States, shall, from and after the passage of this act, be forever free, any law, usage, or custom whatsoever to the contrary notwithstanding."[cxxxix]

In a gesture much too late to be beneficial, the Confederate Congress on March 13, 1865 authorized President Jefferson Davis to recruit slave men as soldiers, with the permission of their owners.

In the spring of 1865, the Union Army of General William T. Sherman marched nearly unchallenged through the Carolinas. The only attempt to halt them came on March 19 when Sherman and the Confederate forces of General Joseph Johnston faced off at the Battle of Bentonville. It was the largest battle ever fought in North Carolina and was the last full-scale tactical offensive mounted in the U.S. Civil War by the Confederate Army. A detachment of the 110th USCI is mentioned as part of Sherman's 4th Division in Bentonville, though unassigned in combat.

The 12th, 13th, 14th, 16th, and some companies of the 110th U.S. Colored Infantries resumed picket, guard, and garrison duty along the Nashville and Northwestern Railroad. The other Abernathy soldiers continued to languish in the Mobile, Alabama prison and would soon bear witness to a deadly twist of fate. Other than **Wesley Rivers** who fled from Forrest's army hours after being captured, only 3 Abernathys spoke of their escapes from prison. **Jefferson (Brunson) Abernathy** deposed, "I escaped in April in company with **Archy Brown** (dead) and rejoined my company at White Bluff Station, TN. I went first from Choctaw Bluff to Nashville where I was forwarded to my command."[cxl] **Lewis Abernathy** (Co. G, 111th USCI) deposed, "As prisoners we were taken to Mobile, Alabama where I remained until I made my escape, in the latter part of April 1865 and went to Selma, Alabama, where I arrived on the day of the surrender in the South. I then joined my company at Mobile in May

1865, remaining there, perhaps, 3 or 4 days, when all the prisoners were sent by boat to New Orleans, Louisiana and thence to Nashville, Tennessee arriving there, I think about June 1st."[cxli]

Even if a soldier could flee from a Confederate prison, he ran the risk of recapture. **Frank Abernathy** (Co. B, 111th USCI) told the notary taking his statement "he was taken prisoner once and recaptured again. He was struck over the head once with a piece of iron by [a] 2nd mate on a steamer and [was] carried off for dead."[cxlii] **Jefferson (Brunson) Abernathy** was also recaptured in May of 1865. **Edmond Reed** said of **Jefferson** and himself, "We were both in prison when the war ended, that is when Lee surrendered."[cxliii]

The pension records of **Frank Abernathy**, **Lewis Abernathy**, and **Ned Abernathy** (Co. K, 110th USCI) mention that these 3 soldiers were wounded by a magazine explosion in Mobile, Alabama. At the close of the Civil War, Federal troops occupied the city. Two hundred tons of shells and gunpowder were stored inside the Beauregard Street warehouse in northeastern Mobile that was used as their ordnance depot. The carelessness of the workers handling live ammunition resulted in cyclical explosions that destroyed 9 city blocks on May 25, 1865. The concussion of the blast was powerful enough to level several houses and sink ships in the Mobile River. The ground rumbled. Bursting shells could be heard throughout the city as they rocketed through the sky and landed indiscriminately on property and passersby. The fires that followed left all of northern Mobile in smoking ruins. An estimated 300 people died and $5 million in property damage was done. **Lewis Abernathy's** wounds were not stated. **Frank Abernathy** who was in the "hospital at Mobile, Alabama since May 25, 1865", suffered a head injury.[cxliv] **Ned Abernathy** was "spitting blood" and was sent to the New Orleans Corps d'Afrique Hospital where he died August 18, 1865 of Phthisis Pulmonalis.[cxlv]

After their release from the Mobile Confederate Prison, the members of the 110th and 111th USCI returned to guard duty along the N&NWRR. Some soldiers were given special assignments and promotions for their fortitude. **Henry Tarpley** was promoted to Sergeant.[cxlvi] **Henry Abernathy** (Co. G, 111th USCI) was promoted to Corporal.[cxlvii] On August 10, 1865, **Harrison Abernathy** was ordered to the Quarter Master's Department in Gallatin.[cxlviii] **Monroe Tarpley** began driving ambulances in September 1865.[cxlix] **Harrison Rivers** became a hospital nurse.[cl] **Frank Abernathy** (Co. C, 111th USCI) was assigned to the Post Headquarters in Murfreesboro, Tennessee.[cli]

From the close of the war until the Infantries' mustering out, the following deaths occurred at Murfreesboro Regimental Hospital: **Giles Abernathy** on August 2, 1865 of typhoid fever,[clii] **Frank Abernathy** (Co. C, 111th USCI) on December 23, 1865 of smallpox,[cliii] and Private **Monroe Tarpley** on April 9, 1866 of consumption.[cliv]

Surviving prison and the explosion, **Lewis Abernathy** still had to face punishment for desertion. The Company Muster Roll for July 1865 read that he was "sentenced by court-martial to two years imprisonment with loss of all pay and allowances during that time for desertion. Presently too sick to be sent to military prison." By September however, **Lewis** had been "restored to duty without the loss of pay or allowances from military prison."[clv]

The former Abernathy, Eason, Rivers, and Tarpley slaves were mustered out at various dates from January to April 1866 in Nashville, Tennessee and Huntsville, Alabama.

VI

Aftermath - Repercussions of the
Body, Heart, and Spirit

The Abernathy, Eason, Rivers, and Tarpley slaves left the Federal Army as free men. Some returned to their former plantation and earned a wage. Many returned long enough to gather their families and venture out into the world. Others never returned to Giles County at all. Others still returned to find their families gone.

"After my discharge, I went back to Giles County, Tennessee near Pulaski. I went to Mrs. Abernathy's and stayed that summer and put in a crop," **Esic (Talley) Abernathy/Albert Cunningham** remembered.[clvi] However his ex-mistress's husband, Andrew Jackson Abernathy, denied employing **Esic**, "I next saw him not long after the close of the Civil War. He came home and I had no use for him and he left."[clvii]

Animosity may have been the cause for Andrew J. Abernathy's false testimony, with him possibly hoping **Esic's** pension would be denied. Because of the war, his estate dwindled and his brother John Seward Abernathy was killed in battle. His brothers, Col. Alfred Harris Abernathy and Dr. Charles Clayton Abernathy, had been prisoners of war. Other family members (Clayton Alfred Eason, Richard F. Abernathy, Thomas C. Abernathy, Dixon Tarpley, James L. Tarpley, and William F. Tarpley) who had served with the Confederate 1st Infantry were forced to retreat from the Battle of Nashville after being soundly defeated and pursued by the Union regiments of their former slaves. Despite the need for farm laborers, the atmosphere in Giles County, TN was decidedly segregated.

To avoid the heavy hand of Congressional Reconstruction, Tennessee ratified a state constitutional amendment abolishing slavery on February 22, 1865. That April, Tennessee ratified the 14th Amendment to the United States Constitution. It became the first formerly Confederate state readmitted to the Union on July 24, 1866. Slavery was dead in America. The remaining states that were slow to mend their ways or acknowledge the rights of all colored persons were divided into 5 military districts for supervision during Reconstruction.

Despite the outward appearance of a changed society, old habits died hard in Giles County. Former Confederate General Nathan Bedford Forrest, who imprisoned many black soldiers of the county, founded the Klu Klux Klan on Christmas Eve 1865 in the town of Pulaski. Its original purpose was to oppose voting rights for blacks and to initiate other measures that would end desegregation. James Polk Abernathy (1849-1920), the 7th son of Charles Clayton Abernathy, was an original member. By 1869, Forrest saw the Klu Klux Klan stray from its mission and grow increasingly violent. He disbanded the original organization, however KKK operations continued. Images of postcards from 1912 featuring photographs of the Klan's birthplace can be found on the internet.

With the changing atmosphere, it is understandable why some black residents opted for new beginnings outside of Giles County. **James John "Jack" Abernathy** deposed, "I went right back to the old place and stayed there about 6 weeks. My owner's family was still living there... I was farming during this time, never did anything else...I think it was in 1882 [when] I came to Texas."[clviii] In 1897, **Jefferson (Brunson) Abernathy** stated, "After the war I lived within six miles of Pulaski until I came to Texas 12 years ago."[clix] Others would also relocate to Ellis County, Texas.

Upon their muster out from the Army, many former slaves exercised their newly found freedom of individuality, shedding the surnames of their former owners. **Jefferson Brunson** recalled, "I went by the name of Brunson until the close of the war. Immediately after coming home from the war my old master told me not to go by his name any longer, but to go by my father's name, that that was the right thing to do. So I have gone by Abernathy ever since."[clx]

George W. Abernathy (born c. 1845) also did a surname switch, "I was going by the name of **George W. Green** until I returned home from the war and my father's name was Abernathy, and he had me change my name to **George Abernathy**, this was the cause of the change in my name."[clxi] **John Rivers** followed suit, "I served in [the] war under [the] name **John Rivers**, I lived with a man before service, whose name was Rivers and I took his name. When I came home from service. I took up residence with my father whose name was **Thomas Givens** and in this way I was soon known by [the] name of **John Givens**. I had no thought of this name ever giving me trouble…My father's residence was at Pulaski, Tennessee, where I had a brother."[clxii]

The soldier who served as **Silot Abernathy** was known later as **Silas Lott**, although this may have been his name all along. It is possible that after giving his name at the time of enlistment, the officers also asked for his owner's surname and then combined the two. His widow's pension application was denied because she remarried; therefore an explanation for the change in his name was never pursued.[clxiii] **John R. Abernathy** was born April 12, between 1845 and 1847 as **John Randall** on "Doc Abernathy's farm", though his pension application records do not reveal the name of his father or mother.

Monroe Abernathy's wife was in the dark as to when he used the alias of **James Monroe**, "I made the pension application as the widow of **James Monroe** as I thought this was his true name, but upon getting the record of my marriage to him I found that we were married under the name of **Monroe Abernathy**."[clxiv] Drew Alston and Spencer Dean of Franklin County, Tennessee deposed, "We were well acquainted with him for about 18 years and know that **James Monroe** and **Monroe Abernathy** was the same man. We also know that he drew his pension under the name of **James Monroe**, but transacted his other business under the name of Abernathy."[clxv]

George Washington Eason also changed his name. **Ralph Holt** of Pulaski remembered, "For a time after his discharge he went by the name **George W. Eason** and **Wash Eason**, then he went away and when he returned here he dropped the name Eason and went by the name **George Washington**."[clxvi]

Through illness, injury, death, impatience, or a change of heart, the dynamic of black families was altered during and after the war. Even if a soldier survived and returned home able-bodied, he could find his family dead or refuged in contraband camps. The harsh and unsanitary conditions of military duty afflicted soldiers for the remainder of their lives. A 3-year tour of duty was a long time for a soldier's wife to wait for her husband's safe return or word of his demise, if she were notified at all. Hope dwindled for some and they moved on with their lives as best they could.

Charlotte Buford, who purported herself a former slave of Thomas E. Abernathy, said of **Thomas Abernathy**, "Before the war, **Tom** had a slave wife **Jane** who had been a Rivers before [the] Abernathys got her. In [the] time of the war, **Jane** went off somewhere, and I have not seen her since."[clxvii] His company mate **Toliver Reders** deposed, "After our muster out we came to Buford's, TN on the same train. **Tom** told me that he went to look for the woman **Jane** that he had cohabited with before the war and found that she had gone off with another man."[clxviii]

His slave wife **Jane (Rivers) Abernathy** reportedly left behind their blind son **Lee Abernathy** and died in 1866. The last two claims however are untrue because in 1870 **Jane** was alive and well, with no other man present in her home besides her son **Lee**.[clxix] She resided in Giles County in very close proximity to other former Abernathy slaves such as **Charles** (born c. 1800), **Joseph** (born c. 1837) and his wife **Mindy**, and **Thom** (born c. 1825).

Whatever the circumstances for their split, **Thomas** did not wait long to find another wife. On August 17, 1867 he wed widow **Maria Carter Dabney Sutton** in Buford's Tennessee. In **Maria's** widow's pension claim she stated, "I got acquainted with **Tom Abernathy** here at Buford's after the war. We were acquainted for about one year before our marriage."[clxx]

The Southern Claims Commission was established to provide monetary relief to those who had property confiscated by the U.S. military for use (horses, livestock, etc.) during the Civil War. In the state of Tennessee, the claim of James Polk Abernathy (7th son of Charles C. Abernathy) was investigated and disallowed, while a claim from the estate of **Braxton Rivers** was declared ineligible and subsequently barred from investigation. The S.C.C. probably felt that as a slave **Braxton Rivers** had no personal property to lose, but at the Abernathy and Rivers plantations, his loss was possible. Since Thomas E. Abernathy was known to give some slaves money, it is plausible that James Rivers learned this practice from his stepfather and in that way **Braxton Rivers** possibly acquired a modest personal estate.

For those who labored, the physical side effects from cruel treatment in the Mobile Confederate prison also took their toll on the families of these black soldiers. **Emma (Dickson) Abernathy**, wife of soldier **Jefferson (Brunson) Abernathy**, spoke of her husband's rheumatism, "He gets so stiff that I have to rub him for hours, and I've seen him unable to lift a cup of coffee to his lips, and has no strength at all in his arms anymore. Many's the day I've plowed to save him when he was not able."[clxxi]   After the log fell on the head of **George W. Abernathe**, he deposed later that the "injury caused a paralysis of the left side or a numbness or want of strength in that side."[clxxii]

A vast majority of the Abernathy, Eason, Rivers, and Tarpley slaves who served in the Union Army would file pension claims or have one filed on their behalf by family members. Proof of age, identity, marital status, military service, and disability or death, all essential in claims processing, were difficult to come by for slaves who were denied legal birth, death, and marriage records. It was at task, at the very least, to locate and have deposed family of former owners, fellow slaves, midwives, and regiment mates would could identify them and swear to their military service and injuries sustained. Because of this, processing of pension claims for black soldiers was delayed or sometimes abandoned when applicants died waiting.

It took at least 4 years for any progress to be made in the claim of **George W. Abernathe**. His situation was so dire and his family so desperate, that one of his daughters wrote to the President of the United States.

N. Topeka, Kansas April 9, 1891.

Hon. Benjamin Harrison, Pres. of U.S.

Dear Sir,

I pen a few lines to your honor to ask a favor of you, hoping very much that you grant my request. My father was a soldier in the late civil war. He was hurt while there. He has applied for a pension a long time ago but has not got it yet. Poor mother has to work so very hard to keep us bread. Now dear Mr. President won't you see why they don't send my pa any money. It has been many years since pa was able to do any work and mother is worked her poor self all most to death. We have 9 in [the] family and times are so very hard. Dear Mister President won't you do this for a poor little child. The reason I write to you is because I know that you have a good and tender heart. Dear Mr. President we are in need. Oh won't you come to our aid. Mr. Harrison I will close hoping that you will answer soon for we are in need. Now Mr. President won't you tell the commission men to give poor papa something. My pa's name is George Abernathe, Co. D, 13th reg. Colored Troops. I am not sure that this is exactly correct, but I think it is. No more at present. Please write soon.

I am yours respectfully,
Joana B. Abernathe
North Topeka, Kans.

Mr. Bishop Crumrine is my father's agent.

Appendix A

African-American Abernathys, Rivers, and Tarpleys in the 1870 Federal Census for Giles County, TN

(Persons described by the Census Takers as "Mulatto" have been **bolded**)

ABERNATHY, Abram (48) b.VA; **Melvina** (32) b. TN; Washington (10); July (13); Sis (4); William B. (1);

ABERNATHY, Alfred (17) b. TN, a domestic servant;

ABERNATHY, Amanda (47); Mariah (16); Watkins (14); Wade (2); Sally (1); July (13);

ABERNATHY, Argen (65) b. VA; Branch (13) b. TN; Harrison (22) b. VA; Sam (26) b. VA; Tony (19) b. VA; Lucy (17) b. VA;

ABERNATHY, **Auston** (63) b. NC, a house carpenter; Francis (27) b. TN; Ann (10); Sarah (6); Joseph (2);

ABERNATHY, Benjamin (25) b. TN; Caroline (30) b. TN;

ABERNATHY, Champ (45) b. VA, a blacksmith; Silla (30) b. TN; **Steven** (9); William (50; Elizabeth (2);

ABERNATHY, Charles (70) b. NC; Klara (70) b. VA;

ABERNATHY, Columbus (47); Tena (39); Betty (16); Malinda (14); General (6); Henry (9); Virginia (2); George A. (1m).

ABERNATHY, Davie (45) b. GA; **Haty** (44) b. TN; Elizabeth (6); Furga (3);

ABERNATHY, Dick (21) b. TN; Julia (21) b. AL; Emeline (1);

ABERNATHY, Eli (30) b. GA; **Elmira** (26) b. TN; Delia (4); Caroline (2);

ABERNATHY, Franklin (70); Mary (70); Lou Ann (17);

ABERNATHY, George (20) b. TN, a farmer; Nellie (18) b. TN;

ABERNATHY, George (50) b. VA, a farmer; Sarah (55) b. TN; Margarette (18); Mildred (16); Jose (9); Hester (8); Georgia (6);

ABERNATHY, H. (35) b. TN, a farmer; Ann (25); Sarah J. (9); Ellen (4); Babe (2); William (11m);

ABERNATHY, Harrison (25) b. VA; Paralee (35) b. TN;

ABERNATHY, Hartwell (55) b. VA; Charlotte (45) b. VA; Robert Buford (19); Mary L. Buford (8);

ABERNATHY, Henry (36); July (27); Patsy (7); James (6); Ada (1m);

ABERNATHY, Jack (55) b. TN, a farmer; ____ (25); C. (14); Andrew (9); John (8m);

ABERNATHY, James (21);

ABERNATHY, James (30); Sophia (24); William (5); John (3);

ABERNATHY, **James** (45) b. TN; **Mary** (43) b. TN; **James** (21) b. TN;

ABERNATHY, James (51) b. TN, a farmer with $1300 real estate; Mary (49) b. NC; Jordan (13) b. TN; Mary (10); Lucy Abernathy (82) b. VA;

ABERNATHY, Jane (40) b. TN; Lee (16) b. TN;

ABERNATHY, Jefferson (25); Emily (20); Robert (1);

ABERNATHY, John (28) b. TN, a cook;

ABERNATHY, Joseph (33); Mindy (28);

ABERNATHY, **July** (70) b. VA; James (25) b. NC; **Caroline James** (30) b. TN; **Henry Abernathy** (13);

ABERNATHY, Lethy (45) b. TN;

ABERNATHY, Luis (40); Mary (30); Sally (17); James (15); Willis (13); Betty (11); John (9); Jane (7); Joe (5);

ABERNATHY, Mahala (51) b. MD; Eda (14) b. TN; Adaline (10);

ABERNATHY, Major (52); **Rebecca** (59); Easter (22); Buckner (21); Frank (17); Abraham (13); Polly (12); Jeff (8); George (6); Thomas (2);

ABERNATHY, Mary (45) b. TN; Rhoda (18); Lethia (19);

ABERNATHY, Mary (49) b. TN; John (25); Mary F. (23); Susan (19); **Will** (4);

ABERNATHY, Molsey (52) b. NC; Henry (13); Sophia (12);

ABERNATHY, Monroe (34) b. TN; Ruth (17); Nancy (1);

ABERNATHY, Moses (57) b. VA; Charlotte (39) b. VA; Ann (19);

ABERNATHY, Peter (39) b. TN; Ann (25); George W. (10); Luis O. (6); Mary (4); Frederick (8m);

ABERNATHY, Reuben (48) b. VA; Martha (27) b. TN; Eliza (17); Ozella (15); Bell (5); Tennessee (11); Francis (6m);

ABERNATHY, Robert (26) b. TN; **Amy** (27) b. MS; Julia Robinson (50) b. MS;

ABERNATHY, Rufus (25); Amy (?);

ABERNATHY, Sherrel (24) b. VA; **Amandy** (25) b. TN; Susan (2m);

ABERNATHY, Stephen (70) b. VA; Edy (69) b. VA; **Katy** (11) b. TN;

ABERNATHY, **Susan** (22); **Mary** (1); **Nelson** (19); **Isabelle** (12);

ABERNATHY, Susan (50) b. TN; Mary (22); Jane (20); Sarah (18); Walter (9); Rob (8);

ABERNATHY, Thom (45) b. TN, a farmer with $350 real estate; ___ (45) b. VA; John (17) b. TN;

ABERNATHY, Thomas (40) b. TN; **Sarah E.** (43); **Queen** (12); **Thomas M.** (11); **Joseph** (8); **Alice** (3); **Claire** (1);

ABERNATHY, Thomas (50) b. VA; Marriah (38) b. TN; Julia (20) b. TN; Lanizo (8) b. AL; James (1) b. TN;

ABERNATHY, Wash (57) b. TN, a farmer; Harriet (52);

ABERNATHY, William (70) b. VA; Kissy (70) b. VA;

ABERNATHY, William (35) b. TN, a house carpenter; **Rhoda Ann** (33) b. TN; **Bettie** (6);

ABERNATHY, W.S. (34) b. TN, a farmer; Eliza (21) b. TN; Mary (5); girl (1m);

RIVERS, **Braxton** (57) b. VA, a farmer, with $5120 real estate; Lucinda (50) b. TN; **Silas** (32); **Alonzo** (30); **Isaac** (26); **Sackey** (20); **Eliza** (19); **Sealy** (6); **Fanny** (18); **Josiah** (4); **Rosa** (1);

RIVERS, Cinda (40) b. TN, a domestic servant; Elizabeth (16); Adaline (13);

RIVERS, David (40) b. TN, a farmer, with $600 personal estate; Fannie (40) b. VA; Francis (21) b. TN;

RIVERS, Harrison (40) b. TN, with $254 personal estate; Sarah (25); Harriet (15); Susan (6m); Clint (8);

RIVERS, Henry (40) b. TN, a farmer, with $235 personal estate; Isabella (25); Henry (6); Andy (2); Charlotte (70) b. VA; Francis (30) b. TN;

RIVERS, Jack (35) b. TN, a farmer; Milly Roberts (30); Henry Roberts (19); **Martin Rivers** (9); Caledon Roberts (9m);

RIVERS, James (30) b. TN; Virginia (44) b. GA; Daniel (13) b. GA; Zachariah (11) b. GA;

RIVERS, John (36) b. TN; Lila (22); Martha (2); Milton Bass (12); Ann Bass (50) b. VA;

RIVERS, Nancy (38) b. MS; Louisa (16); Alfred (30);

RIVERS, William (56) b. TN, a farmer, with $150 personal estate; Sabrie (48); Washington (18) b. LA; Mathias (17) b. LA;

TARPLEY, Henry (40); Sallie (40); Martha (15); Cornelia (120; Henry (3);

TARPLEY, "Oscar" [actually Austin] (29), b. TN, a farmer with $190 personal estate; Mary (24); William (2); Mary (50);

TARPLEY, Wesley (39) b. TN, a farmer, with $225 personal estate; Lucinda (44) b. TN; Elizabeth (13); Della (10);

Appendix B

Outline of the William & Elizabeth Abernathy Family Tree

I.   Clayton Abernathy married _____
- A. Elizabeth Abernathy-Thweatt
- B. Martha Abernathy-Smartt
- C. Turner Abernathy

II.   Alice Abernathy married George Williams
- A. John Williams
- B. Alice Williams-Hopkins
- C. _____ Williams-Pepper
- D. Rebecca Williams-Harwell
- E. Martha Williams-Morris

III.   William Abernathy Jr.

IV.   Jesse Abernathy married Rebecca _____
- A. Dr. Jesse Abernathy
- B. Elizabeth Abernathy-Denty
- C. _____ Abernathy-Webb
- D. Richard C. Abernathy
- E. William F. Abernathy
- F. Burwell Abernathy

V.   Caty Abernathy married Alexander Tarpley
- A. Paschal Tarpley
- B. Ezra Tarpley
- C. John Clayton Abernathy
- D. Ira Tarpley

VI.   Susanna Abernathy married Alan Abernathy
- A. Adne Abernathy-Swanson
- B. Charles C. Abernathy
- C. William Turner Abernathy
- D. Robert Abernathy
- E. Erasmus Abernathy
- F. Benjamin F. Abernathy

G. John O. Abernathy

VII. John Abernathy married Caty Abernathy

    A. William Abernathy

    B. Jesse Abernathy

    C. Charles Clayton Abernathy

    D. Minerva Abernathy-Young

    E. Louisa C. Abernathy-Young

    F. Eliza Abernathy-Stephenson

VIII. Elizabeth Abernathy married Jonathan Drake

    A. Eliza Drake-Young

IX. Charles Clayton Abernathy married Susanna Waddy & Elizabeth H. Dickson

    A. Elizabeth Clayton Abernathy-Daly

    B. Mary Ann Abernathy-Eason

    C. Gilbert Taylor Abernathy

    D. Alfred Harris Abernathy

    E. Maria D. Abernathy-Payne

    F. Susanna Harris Abernathy-May

    G. Dr. Charles Clayton Abernathy

    H. William Allen Abernathy

    I. John Seward Abernathy

    J. Andrew Jackson Abernathy

    K. Caty Abernathy

    L. James Polk Abernathy

    M. Hibernia Abernathy

    N. Ada Elizabeth Abernathy-Amyett

    O. Robert Dickson Abernathy

    P. Delia Taylor Abernathy-Butler

    Q. Charles Moulton Abernathy

    R. Albert Sydney Abernathy

Notes

A Brief History of Giles County, the Abernathys, and Their Holdings

[i] Abernathy, A.J., "A.J. Abernathy's Branch of the Abernathy Family", April 17, 1907 at Pulaski, Tennessee.
[ii] ibid.
[iii] Porch, Deane, "A History of Giles County" in <u>Giles County, Tennessee 1850 Census</u>, 1971.
[iv] Slave Schedules for Giles and other counties, (National Archives Microfilm Publication M432, Roll 902); 7th Census of the United States, 1850 Tennessee; National Archives Building, Washington, DC.
[v] Free Schedules for Giles County, (National Archives Microfilm Publication M432, Roll 879); 7th Census of the United States, 1850 Tennessee; National Archives Building, Washington, DC.
[vi] Slave Schedules for Giles and other counties, (National Archives Microfilm Publication M653, Roll 1282); 8th Census of the United States, 1860 Tennessee; National Archives Building, Washington, DC.
[vii] Free Schedules for Giles County, (National Archives Microfilm Publication M653, Roll 1251); 8th Census of the United States, 1860 Tennessee; National Archives Building, Washington, DC.

The Abernathy, Eason, Rivers, and Tarpley Slaves; Relations with Their Owners and Their Lives on the Plantation

[viii] Deposition of George W. Abernathe; Pension File of George W. Abernathe (Co. D, 13th USC Infantry), invalid application/certificate numbers 605427/520056; Caledonia E. Abernathe widow application /certificate numbers 673135/491123; National Archives Building, Washington, DC.
[ix] Deposition of James J. Abernathy, 6/3/1895 at Marietta, Chickasaw Nation, Indian Territory; Pension File of James J. Abernathy (Co. H, 14th USC Infantry), invalid application/certificate numbers 622073/ 636611; National Archives Building, Washington, DC.
[x] Deposition of Tennessee Scales, 1/27/1890 at Tarpley, Giles County, TN; Pension File of Lewis Abernathy (Co. C, 111th USC Infantry), invalid application/certificate numbers 274527/480164; National Archives Building, Washington, DC.

[xi] Deposition of Andrew J. Abernathy, 3/1/1913 at Pulaski, Giles County, TN; Pension File of Esic Abernathy/Albert Cunningham (Co. C, 12th USC Infantry), invalid application/certificate numbers 1398239/1172392; National Archives Building, Washington, DC.

[xii] Deposition of Sarah Abernathy, 3/1/1913 at Pulaski, Giles County, TN; Pension File of Esic Abernathy/Albert Cunningham, ibid.

[xiii] Deposition of Esic Abernathy/Albert Cunningham, 10/26/1912 at Cripple Creek, Teller County, Colorado; Pension File of Esic Abernathy/Albert Cunningham, ibid.

[xiv] ibid.

[xv] Deposition of Solomon Talley, 3/25/1902 at Cairo, Alexander County, Illinois; Pension File of Isaac Talley (Co. K, 16th USC Infantry & Co. C, 40th USC Infantry), Delilah Talley widow application /certificate numbers 493110/548590; National Archives Building, Washington, DC.

[xvi] ibid.

[xvii] General Affidavit of Lewis Abernathy, 1/29/1880 at Giles County, Tennessee; Pension File of Lewis Abernathy, ibid.

[xviii] Deposition G of Lum Abernathy, 1/27/1890 at Tarpley, Giles County, TN; Pension File of Lewis Abernathy, ibid.

[xix] Deposition of James J. Abernathy, 7/8/1906 at Ardmore, Carter County, OK; Pension File of James J. Abernathy, ibid.

[xx] Letter from J.L. Cardin to L.P. Padgett, 1/29/1914, Pulaski, TN; Pension File of Reuben Abernathy (Co. G, 111th USC Infantry), invalid application/certificate numbers 364340/467573; National Archives Building, Washington, DC.

[xxi] Pension File of Martin Abernathy (Co. F, 110th USC Infantry), Silloy Abernathy widow application/certificate numbers 162024/157024; National Archives Building, Washington, DC.

[xxii] Pension File of Reese Abernathy (Co. F, 110th USC Infantry), Prudence Abernathy widow application/certificate numbers 233116/ 189013; National Archives Building, Washington, DC.

[xxiii] Deposition of James Bass, 9/3/1892 at Pisgah, TN; Pension File of John Rivers (Co. D, 110th USC Infantry), invalid application/ certificate numbers 997098/973589; Delilia Rivers widow application/ certificate numbers 1015713/768033; National Archives Building, Washington, DC.

[xxiv] Pension File of Austin Tarpley (Co. G, 110th USC Infantry), invalid application/certificates numbers 1045760/980432; Mandora Tarpley widow application number 1586543; National Archives Building, Washington, DC.

[xxv] Schedules for Giles County (National Archives Microfilm Publication M593, Roll 1529, Page 73); 9th Census of the United

States, 1870 Tennessee; National Archives Building, Washington, DC.

[xxvi] Deposition of Sarah E. Buchanan, 3/31/1893 at Weakley, Giles County, TN; Pension File of Wesley Tarpley (Co. G, 110th USC Infantry), Jane Tarpley widow application/certificate numbers 508215 /371304; National Archives Building, Washington, DC.

[xxvii] Deposition of James Rivers, July 26, 1875 at Aspen Hill, Giles County, TN; Pension File of Ned Abernathy (Co. K, 110th USC Infantry), Henry Abernathy dependent father application number 171846; National Archives Building, Washington, DC.

[xxviii] Exhibit A, Deposition of Henry Abernathy, 3/1877 at Giles County, TN; Pension File of Ned Abernathy, *ibid.*

[xxix] Exhibit C, Deposition of Gordon Abernathy, 5/18/1877 at Giles County, TN; Pension File of Ned Abernathy, *ibid.*

[xxx] Exhibit A, Deposition of Henry Abernathy, *ibid.*

[xxxi] Deposition of Sarah Abernathy, 5/17/1877 at Giles County, TN; Pension File of Ned Abernathy, *ibid.*

[xxxii] Deposition B of Wesley Rivers, 5/16/1877 at Giles County, TN; Pension File of Ned Abernathy, *ibid.*

[xxxiii] Deposition of Sarah Abernathy, *ibid.*

[xxxiv] Exhibit C, Deposition of Gordon Abernathy, *ibid.*

[xxxv] Exhibit A, Deposition of Henry Abernathy, *ibid.*

[xxxvi] Deposition A of James Oddway, 5/8/1890 at Nashville, Davidson County, TN; Pension File of Robert Abernathy (Co. A, 111th USC Infantry), Amanda Abernathy widow application number 165302, minor application number 583835; National Archives Building, Washington, DC.

[xxxvii] Pension File of Alfred Rivers (Co. D, 111th USC Infantry), invalid application/certificate numbers 694526/498862; National Archives Building, Washington, DC.

[xxxviii] Pension File of Burrell Rivers (Co. D, 111th USC Infantry), Maria Rivers widow pension application/certificate numbers 159639/122831; National Archives Building, Washington, DC.

[xxxix] Pension File of Henry Rivers (Co. B, 110th USC Infantry), invalid application/certificate numbers 491429/466764; Lizzie Rivers widow application/certificate numbers 1011637/770084; National Archives Building, Washington, DC.

[xl] Schedules for Giles County (National Archives Microfilm Publication M593, Roll 529, Page 251); 9th Census of the United States, 1870 Tennessee; National Archives Building, Washington, DC.

[xlii] Pension File of Washington Rivers (Co. B, 110th USC Infantry), Jane Rivers dependent mother application/certificate 345739/ 252951; National Archives Building, Washington, DC.

[xliii] Free Schedules for Giles County (National Archives Microfilm Publication M432, Roll 879, Page 480); and Slaves Schedules for Giles and Other Counties (National Archives Microfilm Publication M432, Roll 902); 7th Census of the United States, 1850 Tennessee; National Archives Building, Washington, DC.

[xliii] Deposition of Ralph Holt, 7/15/1903 at Pulaski, TN; Pension File of George Washington Eason (Co. C, 12th USC Infantry), invalid application/certificate numbers 1105527/1064680, C-2531092; National Archives Building, Washington, DC.

[xliv] Deposition of Edmond S. Killion, 6/10/1903 at Winchester, Arkansas; Pension File of George Washington Eason, *ibid.*

[xlv] *Ibid.*

[xlvi] Pension File of Peter Eason (Co. G, 111th USC Infantry), Mary Eason dependent mother application number 206123; National Archives Building, Washington, DC.

[xlvii] *Ibid.*

[xlviii] Deposition of Patience Meredith, 12/5/1899 at Pulaski, Giles County, TN; Pension File of Henry Eason (Co. E & G, 111th USC Infantry), Patience Meredith widow application/certificate numbers 527480/498249, Mary Eason dependent mother application number 179846; National Archives Building, Washington, DC.

[xlix] *Ibid.*

[l] Deposition of Mary N. Tarpley, 12/6/1899 at Amity, Tennessee; Pension File of Henry Eason, *ibid.*

[li] Deposition of Patience Meredith, 12/5/1899 at Pulaski, Giles County, TN; Pension File of Henry Eason, *ibid.*

[lii] Deposition of Patience Meredith, 12/1/1898 at Pulaski, Giles County, TN; Pension File of Henry Eason, *ibid.*

[liii] Deposition of Patience Meredith, 12/5/1899 at Pulaski, Giles County, TN; Pension File of Henry Eason, *ibid.*

[liv] Deposition of Luke Freeman, 12/7/1899 at Bee, Giles County, TN; Pension File of Henry Eason, *ibid.*

[lv] Deposition of Mary Kimbro, 12/6/1899 at Pulaski, Giles County, TN; Pension File of Henry Eason, *ibid.*

[lvi] Deposition of Susannah Connell, 12/5/1899 at Giles County, TN: Pension of Henry Eason, *ibid.*

[lvii] Deposition of Patience Meredith, 12/5/1899 at Pulaski, Giles County, TN; Pension File of Henry Eason, *ibid.*

[lviii] Slave Schedules for Giles and Other Counties (National Archives Microfilm Publication M653, Roll 1282), 8th Census of the U.S., 1860 Tennessee; Slave Schedules for Giles and Other Counties (National

Archives Microfilm Publication M432, Roll 902), 7th Census for the U.S., 1850 Tennessee; Schedules for Fentress, Franklin, and Giles Counties (National Archives Microfilm Publication M704, Roll 523), 6th Census of the U.S., 1840 Tennessee; National Archives Building, Washington, DC.
[lix] Pension File of Esic Abernathy/Albert Cunningham, *ibid.*

A Call to Arms - Organizing the Regiments

[lx] Deposition A of Esic Abernathy, 10/16/1912, at Cripple Creek, Teller County, Colorado; *ibid.*
[lxi] Deposition B of Sarah Abernathy, 3/1/1913, at Pulaski, Giles County, TN; *ibid.*
[lxii] Deposition of Patience Meredith, 12/5/1899, at Pulaski, Giles County, TN; *ibid.*
[lxiii] Deposition A of James Oddway, 5/8/1890 at Nashville, Davidson County, TN; Pension File of Robert Abernathy, *ibid.*
[lxiv] Deposition B of Reuben Abernathy, 1/4/1890, at Pulaski, Giles County, TN; Pension File of Lewis Abernathy, *ibid.*
[lxv] Deposition of James J. Abernathy, 6/3/1895, at Marietta, Chickasaw Nation, Indian Territory; Pension File of James J. Abernathy, *ibid.*
[lxvi] Deposition A of Esic Abernathy, 10/16/1912, *ibid.*
[lxvii] Deposition of George W. Eason, 6/10/1903, at Winchester, Drew County, Arkansas; Pension File of George Washington Eason, *ibid.*
[lxviii] Compiled Military Service Records of Volunteer Union Soldiers who Served with the United States Colored Troops (National Archives Microfilm Publication M821, Roll 93); National Archives Building, Washington, DC.
[lxix] Deposition A of James Oddway, 5/18/1890, Nashville, Davidson County, TN; *ibid.*
[lxx] Folder 25, Robert Abernathy; Compiled Military Service Records of the 111th U.S. Colored Infantry, Series M-1946; National Archives Building, Washington, DC.
[lxxi] Deposition of Jonas Mark, 1/3/1890, at Lewisburg, Marshall County, TN; Pension File of Lewis Abernathy, *ibid.*
[lxxii] Deposition of Lewis Abernathy, 1/3/1890, near Pulaski, Giles County, TN; Pension File of Lewis Abernathy, *ibid.*

Daily Military Life - Reminders of Home, Non-Combat Injuries/ Fatalities, and the Beginning of an Epidemic

[lxxiii] General Affidavit of Thomas Watkins, 9/22/1892, at Morgan County, AL; Pension File of Monroe Toply (Co. A, 111th USC Infantry), Harriet Foster dependent mother application/certificate numbers 411331/371960; National Archives Building, Washington, DC.

[lxxiv] Exhibit B, Deposition of Frank Reed at Pulaski, Giles County, TN; Pension File of Reese Abernathy, ibid.

[lxxv] Deposition of Mary Kimbro, 12/6/1899 at Pulaski, Giles County, TN; Pension File of Henry Eason, ibid.

[lxxvi] Exhibit A, Deposition of Henry Abernathy, 3/1877, at Giles County, TN; Pension File of Ned Abernathy, ibid.

[lxxvii] ibid.

[lxxviii] Deposition of Neil Brown and Smith Reynolds, 1876 at Giles County, TN; Pension File of Ned Abernathy, ibid.

[lxxix] Deposition of Tony Abernathy & Lewis Walker, 8/15/1873 at Davidson County, TN; Pension File of Peter Eason, ibid.

[lxxx] Letter to Adjutant General's Office in Washington, DC, 3/31/1873, from the Commissioner of Pensions; Pension File of Peter Eason, ibid.

[lxxxi] Deposition of George Abernathe, 8/10/1887, at Shawnee County, Kansas; Pension File of George W. Abernathe, ibid.

[lxxxii] Comrade's Affidavit of Benjamin Jordan, 1/25/1897, at North Topeka, Shawnee County, Kansas; Pension File of George W. Abernathe, ibid.

[lxxxiii] Officer's Affidavit of Henry Gray, 3/3/1897, at Pulaski, Giles County, TN; Pension File of George W. Abernathe, ibid.

[lxxxiv] Letter to the Commissioner of Pensions, Washington, DC from William Duncan, 4/10/1896, at Columbus, Cherokee County, Kansas; Pension File of George W. Abernathe, ibid.

[lxxxv] General Affidavit of Austin Tarpley, 8/28/1895, at Bodenham, TN; Pension File of Austin Tarpley, ibid.

[lxxxvi] Folder 22, Daniel Abernathy; Compiled Military Service Records of the 110th U.S. Colored Infantry; Series M1946; National Archives Building, Washington, DC.

[lxxxvii] Compiled Military Service Records of Volunteer Union Soldiers who Served with the United States Colored Troops (National Archives Microfilm Publication M821, Roll 98); National Archives Building, Washington, DC.

[lxxxviii] Pension File of Grannison Abernathy (Co. D, 110th USC Infantry), James Abernathy dependent father application number 171845; National Archives Building, Washington, DC.

[lxxxix] Deposition A of Jefferson Abernathy alias Brunson, 10/29/1897, at Waxahachie, Ellis County, Texas; Pension File of Jefferson Abernathy, invalid pension/certificate numbers 1097328/825301,

Emma Abernathy widow application/certificate numbers 964498/ 727046; National Archives Building, Washington, DC.

[xc] Pension File of Foster Abernathy (Co. G, 111th USC Infantry), Frank Abernathy dependent father application number 269624; National Archives Building, Washington, DC.

[xci] Pension File of Reese Abernathy (Co. F, 110th USC Infantry), *ibid.*

[xcii] Deposition of Baylor Watson, 6/19/1880, at Giles County, TN; Pension File of Reese Abernathy, *ibid.*

[xciii] Deposition A of Lewis Abernathy, January 3, 1890, near Pulaski, Giles County, TN; Pension File of Lewis Abernathy, *ibid.*

[xciv] Folder 15, Lewis Abernathy; Compiled Military Service Records of the 111th U.S. Colored Infantry, Series M1946; National Archives Building, Washington, DC.

[xcv] Deposition H of Tennessee Scales, 1/28/1890, at Tarpley, Giles County, TN; Pension File of Lewis Abernathy, *ibid.*

[xcvi] Deposition D of Merritt Scales, 1/6/1890, at Pulaski, Giles County, TN; Pension File of Lewis Abernathy, *ibid.*

[xcvii] Deposition A of Lewis Abernathy, January 3, 1890, *ibid.*

[xcviii] Folder 15, Lewis Abernathy, *ibid.*

[xcix] Folder 17, Doctor Abernathy; Compiled Military Service Records of the 110th U.S. Colored Infantry; Series M1946; National Archives Building, Washington, DC.

[c] Deposition of Willis Malone, at Jefferson County, Alabama; Pension File of George W. Abernathy (Co. K, 110th USC Infantry), invalid application number 488410; National Archives Building, Washington, DC.

[ci] Folder 25, Fount Jones; Box 22; Compiled Military Service Records of the 111th USC infantry; Series M1946; National Archives Building, Washington, DC.

The Wages of War - Clashes with the Rebels, Battle Scars, and Prisoners of War

[cii] Declaration for Original Invalid Pension of Wesley Rivers, 4/28/1883; Pension File of Wesley Rivers (Co. K, 110th USC Infantry), invalid application number 486317, Bettie Rivers widow application/certificate numbers 453812/370418; National Archives Building, Washington, DC.

[ciii] Folder 15, Lewis Abernathy, Lewis Abernathy, *ibid.*

[civ] Folder 978, Alfred Rivers; Box 35; Compiled Military Service Records of the 111th U.S. Colored Infantry; Series M1946; National Archives Building, Washington, DC.

[cv] Deposition of Henry Tarpley, 5/15/1894, at Chattanooga, TN; Pension File of Henry Tarpley (Co. G, 111th USC Infantry, invalid

application/certificate numbers 753106/997430; National Archives Building, Washington, DC.

[cvi] Deposition A of James Oddway, 5/8/1890 at Nashville, Davidson County, TN; Pension File of Robert Abernathy, *ibid.*

[cvii] Folder 25, Robert Abernathy; Compiled Military Service Records of the 111th U.S. Colored Infantry; Series M1946; National Archives Building, Washington, DC.

[cviii] Deposition A of James Oddway, 5/8/1890, *ibid.*

[cix] Deposition B of Peyton Black, 5/8/1890, at Nashville, Davidson County, TN; Pension File of Robert Abernathy, *ibid.*

[cx] Folder 25, Robert Abernathy, *ibid.*

[cxi] *ibid.*

[cxii] Deposition A of Reuben Abernathy, 1/22/1890, at Tarpley, Giles County, TN; Pension File of Reuben Abernathy (Co. G, 111th USC Infantry), invalid application/certificate numbers 364340/467573; National Archives Building, Washington, DC.

[cxiii] Comrade Testimony of Lewis Abernathy, 5/12/1888; Pension File of Reuben Abernathy, *ibid.*

[cxiv] General Affidavit of Reuben Abernathy, 1/5/1898; Pension File of Reuben Abernathy, *ibid.*

[cxv] Deposition A of Lewis Abernathy, 1/3/1890, *ibid.*

[cxvi] Affidavit of John Rivers, 2/16/1895, at Giles County, TN; Pension File of John Rivers, *ibid.*

[cxvii] Surgeon's Certificate of Examination, 8/24/1898 in Cleveland, Bradley County, TN; Pension File of Henry Tarpley, *ibid.*

[cxviii] Deposition of Willis Malone, at Jefferson County, Alabama; Pension File George W. Abernathy, *ibid.*

[cxix] Deposition of Jefferson Abernathy, 10/29/1897, *ibid.*

[cxx] Neighbor's Affidavit of Peter Kinder, 3/27/1891, at Pulaski, Giles County, TN; Pension File of Monroe Abernathy (Co. F, 110th USC Infantry), invalid application number 1009411; Desdy Abernathy widow application/certificate numbers 612876/452915; National Archives Building, Washington, DC.

[cxxi] Affidavit of Daniel McTaggart, 4/5/1866, at Murfreesboro, TN; Pension File of Frederick Abernathy (Co. G, 111th USC Infantry), Melissa Abernathy widow application/certificate numbers 1087631/ 91003; National Archives Building, Washington, DC.

[cxxii] Deposition of Thomas Butler and Tyler Abernathy, Giles County, TN; Pension File of Martin Abernathy, *ibid.*

[cxxiii] Deposition B of Wesley Rivers, 5/16/1877, at Giles County, TN; Pension of Ned Abernathy, *ibid.*

[cxxiv] Folder 1100, David Tarpley; Box 41; Compiled Military Service Records of the 111th USC Colored Infantry; Series M1946; National Archives Building, Washington, DC.

[cxxv] Folder 110, Monroe Tarpley; Box 41; Compiled Military Service Records of the 111th USC Colored Infantry; Series M1946; National Archives Building, Washington, DC.

[cxxvi] Deposition of Robert Abernathy, 6/19/1901, at Buford, TN; Pension File of Thomas Abernathy (Co. F, 110th USC Infantry), invalid application/certificate numbers 788072/835507, Maria Abernathy widow application/certificate numbers 697931/516591; National Archives Building, Washington, DC.

[cxxvii] Deposition A of Payne Harris, 9/23/1895, at Murfreesboro, Rutherford County, TN; Pension File of James J. Abernathy, *ibid.*

[cxxviii] Deposition of James J. Abernathy, 6/3/1895, at Marietta, Chickasaw Nation, Indian Territory; Pension File of James J. Abernathy, *ibid.*

[cxxix] Deposition A of Payne Harris, 9/23/1895, at Murfreesboro, Rutherford County, TN; Pension File of James J. Abernathy, *ibid.*

[cxxx] Deposition of James J. Abernathy, 6/3/1895, at Marietta, Chickasaw Nation, Indian Territory, *ibid.*

[cxxxi] Deposition of George W. Eason, 6/10/1903, at Winchester, Drew County, Arkansas; Pension File of George W. Eason, *ibid.*

[cxxxii] Report of Major General George H. Thomas, U.S. Army, Commanding Dept. of the Cumberland, Battle of Nashville, written 1/20/1865 in Eastport, MS to Lieutenant Colonel R.M. Sawyer, Assistant Adjunct General, Military Division of the Mississippi.

[cxxxiii] General Affidavit of James Monroe, 5/27/1889, at Crawford, Arkansas; Pension File of Monroe Abernathy alias James Monroe (Co. D, 13th USC Infantry), invalid application/certificate numbers 708192/678498, Ruthy Monroe widow application/certificate numbers 799418/588382; National Archives Building, Washington, DC.

[cxxxiv] General Affidavit of William Duncan, 7/24/1889, at Osage County, Kansas; Pension File of Monroe Abernathy alias James Monroe, *ibid.*

[cxxxv] Compiled Military Service Records of Volunteer Union Soldiers who Served with the United States Colored Troops (National Archives Microfilm Publication M1821, Roll 78); National Archives Building, Washington, DC.

[cxxxvi] Deposition A of Esic Abernathy, October 16, 1912, Cripple Creek, Teller County, Colorado, *ibid.*

[cxxxvii] Report of Major General James B. Steedman, U.S. Army, Commanding Provisional Detachment (District of the Etowah), The Battle of Nashville, Chattanooga, TN, 1/27/1865, to Brig. General W.D. Whipple, Chief of Staff.

[cxxxviii] Deposition of James J. Abernathy, 6/3/1895, at Marietta, Chickasaw Nation, Indian Territory, *ibid.*

[cxxxix] "A Resolution to Encourage and Promote the Efficiency of the Military Forces of the United States", p. 571, Volume 13, (Boston, 1866); U.S. Statutes at Large, Treaties, and Proclamations of the United States.

[cxl] Deposition A of Jefferson Abernathy, 10/29/1897, at Waxahachie, Ellis County, Texas, *ibid.*

[cxli] Deposition A of Lewis Abernathy, 1/3/1890, near Pulaski, Giles County, TN; Pension File of Lewis Abernathy, *ibid.*

[cxlii] Letter to the Commissioner of Pensions from Frank Abernathy, 9/1922, at Bee Branch, Van Buren County, Arkansas; Pension File of Frank Abernathy (Co. B, 111th USC Infantry), invalid application/ certificate numbers 828536/980446, Idella Abernathy widow application number 613345; National Archives Building, Washington, DC.

[cxliii] Deposition of Edmond Reed, 2/24/1898, at Tarpley, Giles County, TN; Pension File of Jefferson Abernathy, *ibid.*

[cxliv] Folder 22, Frank Abernathy; Compiled Military Service Records of the 111th USC Infantry; Series M-1946; National Archives Building, Washington, DC.

[cxlv] Folder 27, Ned Abernathy; Compiled Military Service Records of the 110th USC Infantry; Series M-1946; National Archives Building, Washington, DC.

[cxlvi] Folder 1101, Henry Tarpley; Box 41; Compiled Military Service Records of the 111th USC Infantry; Series M-1946; National Archives Building, Washington, DC.

[cxlvii] Folder 14, Henry Abanatha; Compiled Military Service Records of the 111th USC Infantry; Series M-1946; National Archives Building, Washington, DC.

[cxlviii] Folder 25, Harrison Abernathy; Compiled Military Service Records of the 111th USC Infantry; Series M-1946; National Archives Building, Washington, DC.

[cxlix] Folder 1102, Monroe Tarpley; Box 41; Compiled Military Service Records of the 111th USC Infantry; Series M-1946; National Archives Building, Washington, DC.

[cl] Folder 980, Harrison Rivers; Box 35; Compiled Military Service Records of the 111th USC Infantry; Series M-1946; National Archives Building, Washington, DC.

[cli] Folder 23, Frank Abernathy; Compiled Military Service Records of the 111th USC Infantry; Series M-1946; National Archives Building, Washington, DC.

[clii] Folder 24, Giles Abernathy; Compiled Military Service Records of the 111th USC Infantry; Series M-1946; National Archives Building, Washington, DC.

[cliii] Folder 23, Frank Abernathy, *ibid.*

[cliv] Folder 1102, Monroe Tarpley; Box 41, *ibid.*

[clv] Folder 15, Lewis Abernathy; Compiled Military Service Records of the 111th USC Infantry; Series M-1946; National Archives Building, Washington, DC.

Aftermath - Repercussions of the Body, Heart, and Spirit

[clvi] Deposition of Esic Abernathy, 10/16/1912, at Cripple Creek, Teller County, Colorado; *ibid.*

[clvii] Deposition of Andrew J. Abernathy, 3/1/1913, at Pulaski, Giles County, TN; *ibid.*

[clviii] Deposition of James J. Abernathy, 6/3/1895, *ibid.*

[clix] Deposition of Jefferson Abernathy alias Brunson, 10/29/1897, *ibid.*

[clx] *Ibid.*

[clxi] General Affidavit of George W. Abernathy, 4/20/1898, at Bessemer, Jefferson Count, Alabama; Pension File of George W. Abernathy, *ibid.*

[clxii] General Affidavit of John Rivers, 3/30/1891, at Gibson County, Indiana; Pension File of John Rivers (alias John T. Givens) Co. A 14th USC Infantry, invalid application/certificate numbers 764066/ 738123, Anna Givens widow application number 1140704; National Archives Building, Washington, DC.

[clxiii] Pension File of Silot Abernathy, (Co. F, 16th USC Infantry), Mary J. Stowers widow application #543896; National Archives Building, Washington, DC.

[clxiv] General Affidavit of Ruthy Abernathy, 1/2/1905, at Franklin County, Tennessee; Pension File of Monroe Abernathy alias James Monroe, *ibid.*

[clxv] General Affidavit of Drew Alston and Spencer Dean, 1/2/1905, at Franklin County, Tennessee; Pension File of Monroe Abernathy alias James Monroe, *ibid.*

[clxvi] Deposition A of Ralph Holt, 7/15/1903, at Pulaski, Giles County, Tennessee, Pension File of George W. Eason, *ibid.*

[clxvii] Deposition of Charlotte Buford, 6/19/1901, at Buford's, Giles County, Tennessee; Pension File of Thomas Abernathy, *ibid.*

[clxviii] Deposition of Toliver Reders, 6/9/1901, at Buford's, Giles County, TN; Pension File of Thomas Abernathy, *ibid.*

[clxix] Schedules for Giles County (National Archives Microfilm Publication M593, Roll 1529); 9th Census of the United States, 1870 Tennessee; National Archives Building, Washington, DC.

[clxx] Deposition of Maria Abernathy, 6/19/1901, at Buford's, Giles County, TN; Pension File of Thomas Abernathy, *ibid.*

[clxxi] Deposition of Mrs. Emma Abernathy, 10/29/1897, at Waxahachie, Ellis County, Texas; Pension File of Jefferson Brunson/ Abernathy, *ibid*.
[clxxii] Deposition of George W. Abernathe, 8/10/1887, at Shawnee County, Kansas; Pension File of George W. Abernathe, *ibid*.

Index

(Names in parentheses are former slave surnames. Bolded names are African-American.)

Harriet (Bass), 17
Harrison, 19, 33, 71
Hartwell, 11
Hartwell, 19
Henry, 19, 21, 22, 33, 40, 52, 71
Henry (Talley), 15, 33
Henry (Brunson), 16
Isabelle, 19
Isham, 19
Jack, 19
James, 19, 43
James John "Jack", 13, 16, 33, 35, 61, 64, 67, 75
James Polk, 74, 78
Jane (Rivers), 77-78
Jeff, 19
Jefferson (Brunson), 16, 33, 34, 43, 44, 52, 58, 69, 75, 79
Jennie (Rivers), 22
Jesse, 7, 9
Jesse, 16, 33
John, 7, 9, 11, 29,
John, 19, 33, 76
John Clayton, 11
John Seward, 73
Joseph, 9,
Joseph, 19, 78
Julie, 19
Kissy, 19
Lee, 78
Lethia, 19
Lewis, 15-16, 33-34, 37, 44-45, 52, 57, 69-71
Liles, 9
Lillie, 19
Lizzie, 13
Lou Ann, 19
Louisa (Rivers), 22
Lucy, 16, 19
Luis, 19
Mahala, 19
Major, 19
Malinda (Brunson), 16
Manuel, 33
Margaret, 22
Maria (Carter/Dabney) Sutton, 78
Maria (Ordway), 23

Martha, 9
Martha (Ordway), 23
Martha Paine-Rivers, 11, 21
Martin, 17, 33, 59
Mary, 11
Mary,13, 19, 26, 29
Mary Frances (Bass), 17
Mason (Rivers), 22
Mat, 10
May,19
Melissa (Tarpley), 20
Mildred, 19
Milly, 19
Milton, 10
Mindy, 78
Mira, 22
Molsey, 19
Monroe, 20, 33, 52, 58, 65, 76
Moses, 20
Nancy, 22
Narcissie (Osborne), 18
Ned, 22, 33, 40, 52, 60, 70
Nelson, 20
Parthenia (Brunson), 16
Peter, 20
Phebe, 18
Polly, 20
Priestly (Bass), 17
Prudence Martha (Osborne), 17-18, 40
Rebecca, 22
Reese, 17-18, 40, 44
Reuben, 17, 20, 33, 35, 44, 53, 56-57
Rhoda, 20
Richard, 10, 73
Richard, 20, 33, 52, 59
Robert, 10, 11, 29,
Robert, 20, 22, 33, 35-36, 53-56, 60
Robert (Bass), 17
Roeny, 45
Ruff/Rufus, 20, 60-61
Sam, 20
Samuel, 10
Sarah, 20, 22
Sarah (Bass), 17

Sarah Elizabeth Talley, 14, 30
Sherrell, 20
Silloy/Susan (Bass), 17, 59
Silot, 15, 33, 76
Sophia, 20
Sophia (Rivers), 22
Squire, 20
Stephen, 20
Sterling, 9, 11
Susan, 20
Susanna, 7
Sylvester, 20
Tennessee, 13, 16, 44-45
Thomas, 20, 52, 60, 77
Thomas, 73
Thomas E., 7, 9-11, 21, 22, 23, 29, 35, 60, 78
Tom (Rivers), 22
Tony, 20, 33, 41, 52
Turner, 11, 29
Tyler, 22, 33, 52, 59
Walter (Bass), 17
Wash, 20
Watkins (Ordway), 23
Wilkins, 10
William, 7, 9, 10, 11
William, 20
William Reese, 33
William Sylvester, 20, 33
Adams,
    Abe/Amos, 34
    Bettie, 34
Alabama,
    Athens, 37, 40, 44, 46, 51, 52, 60
    Decatur, 61, 66
    Elkmont, 37
    Florence, 54
    Huntsville, 66, 72
    Larkinsville, 66
    Mobile, 54, 58, 59, 60, 69, 70
    Selma, 69
Alston, Drew, 76
Bass,
    Ann (House), 18
    Burrell, *see Burrell (Bass) Abernathy*

104

106

Nashville & Chattanooga Railroad, 63
Nashville & Decatur Railroad, 37
Nashville & Northwestern Railroad,
    extension by Colored Troops, 35-36, 62
    guard duty performed by Colored Troops, 36, 41, 71
Sulphur Branch Trestle Railroad Bridge, 36-37, 44
Randall, John, *see John Abernathy*
Reconstruction, 74
Reders, Toliver, 77
Reed,
    Edmond, 70
    Frank, 40
Reese, William, *see Reese Abernathy*
Reynolds, Smith, 40
Rivers,
    Adaline, 25
    Alfred (Huey/Dobbins), 25, 33, 52
    Alonzo, 25
    Braxton, 25, 78-79
    Burrell, 33, 52, 59
    Charlotte, 24
    Cinda, 25
    David, 25
    Delilia (Bass), 18
    Eliza, 25
    Elizabeth, 25
    Fannie, 25
    Francis, 25
    Frankie, 25
    Harrison, 25, 33, 52, 71
    Henry, 24, 30, 33
    Isaac, 25
    Isabella (Flournoy), 24
    Jack, 25
    James, 25
    James W., 21, 24, 29, 78
    Jane (Kemp/Flournoy), 24
    John, 18, 24, 30, 33, 52, 57, 75
    Julia, 24
    Julia Flournoy, 24
    Laura, 24, *see also Laura (Rivers) Powell*
    Lea, 25
    Louisa, 25
    Lucinda, 25